C000050559

Conversations with Joan Didion

Literary Conversations Series
Monika Gehlawat
General Editor

Conversations with Joan Didion

Edited by Scott F. Parker

University Press of Mississippi / *Jackson*

www.upress.state.ms.us

The University Press of Mississippi is a member of
the Association of American University Presses.

Copyright © 2018 by University Press of Mississippi
All rights reserved
Manufactured in the United States of America

First printing 2018
∞

Library of Congress Cataloging-in-Publication Data

Names: Parker, Scott F., editor.
Title: Conversations with Joan Didion / edited by Scott F. Parker.
Description: Jackson: University Press of Mississippi, [2018] | Series:
    Literary conversations series | Includes index. |
Identifiers: LCCN 2017038043 (print) | LCCN 2017038626 (ebook) | ISBN
    9781496815521 (epub single) | ISBN 9781496815538 (epub institutional) |
    ISBN 9781496815545 (pdf single) | ISBN 9781496815552 (pdf institutional)
    | ISBN 9781496815514 (hardback)
Subjects: LCSH: Didion, Joan—Interviews. | Novelists, American—20th
    century—Interviews. | BISAC: BIOGRAPHY & AUTOBIOGRAPHY / Literary. |
    LITERARY COLLECTIONS / American / General. | LITERARY CRITICISM / American
    / General.
Classification: LCC PS3554.I33 (ebook) | LCC PS3554.I33 Z46 2018 (print) |
    DDC 818/.5409 [B]—dc23
LC record available at https://lccn.loc.gov/2017038043

British Library Cataloging-in-Publication Data available

Works by Joan Didion

Nonfiction

Slouching Towards Bethlehem (1968)
The White Album (1979)
Salvador (1983)
Miami (1987)
After Henry (1992)
Political Fictions (2001)
Fixed Ideas: America Since 9.11 (2003)
Where I Was From (2003)
The Year of Magical Thinking (2005)
We Tell Ourselves Stories in Order to Live: Collected Nonfiction (2006)
Blue Nights (2011)
South and West: From a Notebook (2017)

Fiction

Run, River (1963)
Play It As It Lays (1970)
A Book of Common Prayer (1977)
Democracy (1984)
The Last Thing He Wanted (1996)

Screenplays (all with John Gregory Dunne)

The Panic in Needle Park (1971)
Play It As It Lays (1972)
A Star Is Born (1976) (also with Frank Pierson, William A. Wellman, and Robert Carson)
True Confessions (1981)
Up Close and Personal (1996)

Plays

The Year of Magical Thinking (2006)

Contents

Introduction

The seventeen interviews collected here span four decades of Joan Didion's career. It might have been more, but Didion's first two books—*Run River,* her most conventional novel, and *Slouching Towards Bethlehem,* her collection of essays now considered groundbreaking—weren't widely regarded upon publication. Didion's first substantial interview wasn't conducted until 1972, after the publication of the novel *Play It As It Lays* established her as a powerful voice of societal ennui. Neither she nor her husband, the writer John Gregory Dunne, anticipated the success of that book. As Didion recounts to Sheila Heti in 2012, Dunne told her, "This isn't going to—you're never going to—you're never going to—this book isn't going to make it."

But the book did make it—Didion and Dunne would later adapt *Play It As It Lays* for the screen. From her fourth book, the novel *A Book of Common Prayer* (1977), interviews with Didion, selectively granted, began to appear in notable clusters around the publications of her books. The first, and most significant, such cluster came in 1977. In these interviews we see women interviewers looking to unpack the mystique of coolness and casual sophistication that has already crept up around Didion. They examine the dynamics of her marriage and the similarities between Didion and her characters. Before Susan Braudy interviews Didion for *Ms.,* Gloria Steinem instructs her to "ask her why she always writes about masochists, nonfunctioning women, when she herself is such a tough, highly functioning writer." Didion never accepts such a neat distinction. Speaking of Charlotte Douglas from *A Book of Common Prayer,* she tells Sara Davidson in the *New York Times Book Review,* "Obviously the book finds her at a crisis. I don't know too many people who have what you could call clearly functioning centers." This "void at the center of experience," as she refers to it in her interview with Susan Stamberg for *All Things Considered,* is a recurring theme in Didion's work, the first example of a narrative that collapses under her critical eye.

Not only is the concept of self ultimately hollow for Didion, so is the concept of women as a category. She resists belonging to any class narrower than "writer." Her scathing 1972 essay "The Women's Movement" is at least as troubling to readers who want to see Didion as an icon of second-wave feminism as is her fiction. As recently as 2011, Terry Gross asks Didion if during the sixties and seventies she had been trying to figure out her dual roles as mother and writer. Didion says, "It never crossed my mind that I would have to figure it out. I always thought I would be working. And I always thought I would have a baby if I was lucky enough. So I wasn't as troubled by that."

Didion is dispositionally opposed to movements. Returning to her interview with Stamberg: "I am a moralist, but I grew up in such a strong West Coast ethic that I tend not to impose my own sense of what is wrong and what is right on other people. If I do impose it, I feel very guilty about it, because it is entirely against the ethic in which I was brought up, which was strictly *laissez-faire*." Though she will come to see the cracks in this narrative too, Western-style individualism remains at the core of her worldview.

When a second generation of women writers embrace Didion (in addition to Heti's interview included here, Didion has been interviewed by Meghan Daum, Sloane Crosley, and Vendela Vida), it is as a respected elder, a status earned in part by her having been a fixture of the political vanguard, whether or not she meant do anything more than write well.

While her status as a feminist icon is complicated, her status as a preeminent essayist is perfectly straightforward. When the *Paris Review* began its Art of Nonfiction series in 2006, Didion was the first writer they spoke with (Linda Kuehl had already interviewed her for their longstanding Art of Fiction in 1978). This interview with Hilton Als belongs to the biggest wave of Didion's interviews, the one that coincided with her most recent books, the memoirs *The Year of Magical Thinking* and *Blue Nights,* which recount the deaths, respectively, of her husband and her daughter, Quintana Roo, and which have allowed her to develop a more personal relationship with her readers. As she tells Als, "I have been getting a very strong emotional response to *Magical Thinking.* But it's not a crazy response; it's not demanding. It's people trying to make sense of a fairly universal experience that most people don't talk about. So this is a case in which I have found myself able to deal with the response directly." Just before this period, in 2003, Didion, in responding to *Vanity Fair*'s Proust Questionnaire (not included here), says, "What strikes me about myself is not my thinness but a certain remoteness." That remoteness, so much a part of her popular image, is layered over in her memoirs and the interviews associated with them by a more accessible personality that accounts in large measure for the resurgence of popular interest in her work.

The relative dearth of interviews from the eighties and nineties tracks with Didion's influence, the books of this period being largely overshadowed by the monumental works that come before and after.

Joan Didion "is not what one would call a virtuoso conversationalist," Davidson warns us. Her conversation style can be halting and repetitive (though she is far less inarticulate than she insists she is). Dave Eggers alludes to this awkwardness in his 2003 interview, when he describes his strategy of putting her at ease by trying "to keep the mood buoyant and conversational." He had noticed that "she seemed to prefer to chat than to be asked to expound. Ponderous, open-ended questions . . . were not going to work."

This approach conforms to what we know about Didion from her writing, too: that she does "not think in abstracts," but attends "to the specific, to the tangible." Ever the empiricist, Didion tells Kuehl, by way of reference to Henry James, that ideas are trouble when they're removed from physical facts. A caution that would be well put to many of her interviewers, who are flummoxed by their inability to locate the fierce writer they know in the diminutive woman before them. Didion, for one, is "not very interested in psychic cause and effect. In why I am the way I am and why you are the way you are." She focuses on surfaces because surfaces are available to her. And it is when she has examined our myths (of the sixties, of California, of New York, of American politics, to name some of the best-known examples) as they relate to the observable facts rather than through them as self-evident stories we live by that so many of them have collapsed under her pen.

All along, her interview responses correspond with her writing—the convincing support for her claim in "Why I Write" that she writes to find out what she knows is how often she actually quotes her own work—but the most striking thread throughout the interviews is Didion's frequent return to the loss, falsity, and breakdown of all narratives, which for Didion are constructions invented by and for us, that work only until they don't.

From her first interview, with Sally Davis, Didion is already referring to the "meaninglessness of experience." Her best-known fictional character, Maria Wyeth from *Play It As It Lays*, tells us, "I know what nothing means, and I keep on playing." This is Joan Didion as avatar of existentialism. All of our narratives fail us, yet we go on. In her 2011 interview with David Ulin, Didion points to living with certain annihilation as the great question of all religions. But rather than offer a response, she ends the interview "on that note."

Before she wanted to be a writer, Didion wanted to be an actor. And as she tells Heti, writing is a kind of acting, only the writer performs herself. Giving an interview, too, is a kind of performance. Didion is careful with what she discloses in these conversations, seemingly operating with her own famous caution from the preface to *Slouching Towards Bethlehem* in mind that writers are always selling someone out. She denies her interviewers the power to define the narrative of Joan Didion. Telling that story has always been her job. The narrative might be false, she would be the first to admit, but it's hers.

Didion is known for her ability to disclose loads of personal information while simultaneously keeping readers at a distance. These interviews do not collapse that distance, but they do alter it, showing Didion in a plainer light than she shines on herself in her prose.

I was limited in what I could include here by my budget and a couple of reluctant copyright holders. The only other exclusions were made to minimize overlap of content. In those interviews that I have transcribed from audio recordings (Swaim, Bernstein, Gross, Ulin) I have silently elided hesitations and falsely started sentences, and in the case of Ulin, also readings Didion was asked to give from her work. The other interviews appear as they were originally published.

SFP

Chronology

1934	Born December 5 in Sacramento, California, to Frank and Eduene Didion.
1941–1943	Family moves to Tacoma, Washington, Durham, North Carolina, and Colorado Springs, Colorado, following Frank's military assignments, before returning to Sacramento.
1955	Wins guest editor position at *Mademoiselle* in New York.
1956	Graduates from the University of California, Berkeley.
1956	Wins *Vogue* essay contest and job at the magazine in New York.
1963	The novel *Run River* is published.
1964	Marries John Gregory Dunne, moves to Los Angeles.
1966	Didion and Dunne adopt newborn Quintana Roo Dunne.
1968	The essay collection *Slouching Towards Bethlehem* is published.
1970	The novel *Play It As It Lays* is published.
1971	The film *The Panic in Needle Park* is released, co-written by Didion and Dunne. Family moves to Malibu.
1972	The film adaptation of *Play It As It Lays* is released, co-written by Didion and Dunne.
1976	The film *A Star Is Born,* co-written by Didion, Dunne, and others is released.
1977	The novel *The Book of Common Prayer* is published.
1978	Family moves to Brentwood Park, Los Angeles.
1979	The essay collection *The White Album* is published.
1981	The film adaptation of Dunne's novel *True Confessions* is released, co-written by Didion and Dunne.
1983	The nonfiction work *Salvador* is published.
1984	The novel *Democracy* is published.
1987	The nonfiction work *Miami* is published.
1988	Didion and Dunne move back to New York.
1992	The essay collection *After Henry* is published.
1996	The novel *The Last Thing He Wanted* is published.

Conversations with Joan Didion

The Female Angst

Sally Davis / 1972

Recorded 1972, broadcast on KPFK February 10, 1972. © 1972 by Pacifica Radio Archives. Reprinted by permission.

Sally Davis: Joan Didion has written, in addition to a vast body of nonfiction for the *Saturday Evening Post* and other American magazines, two novels, and has published a collection of her best nonfiction pieces, *Slouching Towards Bethlehem*. She writes of the confusion and awfulness of modern life; of death by violence, murder, rattlesnake bites, terrible acts of God, evil winds, and the inability of things to hold at the center; the universal falling apart. She has been called this generation's supreme chronicler of angst, she has the ability to show us her own personal pain and in so doing mirror—in the way that Anaïs Nin was talking about earlier[1]—the savagery of nature while shielding us from it. This is a piece from *Play It As It Lays*:

> In January there were poinsettias in front of all the bungalows between Melrose and Sunset, and the rain set in, and Maria wore not sandals but real shoes and a Shetland sweater she bought in New York the year she was nineteen. For days during the rain she did not speak out loud or read a newspaper, she couldn't read newspapers because certain stories leapt at her from the page: the four-year-olds in the abandoned refrigerator, the tea party with Purex, the infant in the driveway, rattlesnake in the playpen, the peril, unspeakable peril, in the everyday. She grew faint as the procession swept before her, the children alive when last scolded, dead when next seen, the children in the locked car burning, the little faces, helpless screams. The mothers were always reported to be under sedation. In the whole world there was not as much sedation as there was instantaneous peril.

Joan, *The National Review*, in one of their reviews of . . . I think it was *Slouching Towards Bethlehem* . . . said of you: "She's passed beyond optimism and pessimism to a far country of quiet anguish, bringing the scant comfort." I wonder what the sources of that anguish are chiefly, and how much of it has to do with being a woman.

Joan Didion: Oh, I don't think any of it does, and I don't know—I don't think of myself as an anguished person particularly. But I'm not optimistic and I'm not pessimistic. The way I think doesn't seem to me to have a great deal specifically to do with being a woman. I wasn't brought up too terribly aware of any kind of special woman's role. I mean, it just never occurred to me that anything would be expected of me other than doing whatever I wanted to do. And I don't feel very specifically aware of women's anguish as opposed to general anguish, to the anguish of being a human being.

SD: Well, I know that you write about the anguish, for instance, of war and the anguish of the human condition as manifested in things like Haight-Ashbury and the drug culture and so on—but very often your metaphors, if you like, for the general angst that goes on in you are female ones. For instance, you're talking about, at one point in *Slouching Towards Bethlehem,* going over the edge into some kind of loss of control, some kind of madness, which shows itself with the sardine tins in the sink and the general slovenliness of the house, which is a kind of a very female concept.

JD: Well, that comes up because, you know, I am a woman and so I do think the images that come to a woman's mind tend to be female, I suppose, and I write women with more facility than I write men, and that's how that happens. But I don't—I did write a man once that I liked, I mean I wrote a man once in my first novel, who I was as close to as the woman in that novel, although the woman was the main character, and I thought that he came off as well as the woman, but it was the only time I've ever really gotten into a man's—

SD: Psyche.

JD: Yeah.

SD: Maria, in *Play It As It Lays* is almost the story of a kind of chronicle of anguish and fear, which strikes me as being—her anguish is particularly female, particularly concerning her daughter and the feelings about her daughter and her abortion and all of those images, all of the manifestations of her fear are particularly female ones.

JD: Well, one of the things I was interested in in that book, I mean one of the things that started coming out of it as I was writing it was the kind of chain of—I mean this isn't what the book was about, but one of the things that kept coming was that kind of chain between generations of women, between Maria and her daughter, and when she was particularly concerned about her daughter and about aborting the child, I found her thinking naturally about her mother. I mean, it seemed to me to be some kind of chain of things understood by women that comes down, but that I don't know what that means.

SD: She's a particularly California kind of type. Her problems are particularly California ones and her way of coping with them like, you know, working out how she's going to negotiate the freeways every day and so on. And I wondered about, if you feel particularly sensitive towards the pains and the difficulties of living, why you would choose to live your life in California where those difficulties seem to be immensely intensified.

JD: Well, I was born in California and lived in New York for eight years, and then after I was married, we moved to Los Angeles, which is a very different place from the place where I come from. And, well, I could only talk about it in two ways. One is that I find it easier to live here, I mean easier in physical terms. I like living here. The other is, that if there is, if there is a place that is—if there is a place in the world that seems to me more real than any other place, I would rather be living there. California in many ways, or Los Angeles in many ways, strikes me as a very—I feel very close to the reality of something here, where I ceased feeling that way in New York.

SD: What kind of reality are you talking about?

JD: What Maria's going through in that book is that she's coming to terms with the meaninglessness of experience, and that's what everybody who lives in Los Angeles essentially has to come to terms with because none of it seems to mean anything.

SD: Is it kind of confronting the worst that there is and then being able to cope with anything else that comes along?

JD: Yeah, I would think that is what people ought to do—yeah.

SD: Because Dory Previn, of course, who is also on this program, feels pretty much the way you do that, I mean for her reality is even more important because the grasp on reality is harder for her to maintain, and she maintains that this is the only place that she can feel it.

JD: Feel it, yeah. I would find it very difficult to live in a sheltered way because I would keep feeling that I was missing the point.

SD: As you said, you're not optimistic, and you're not pessimistic, but you obviously have enough sensitivity to grasp that life is essentially, as you say, "meaningless," if you like. Do you then seek out subjects to intensify this, to show this meaninglessness? I mean, for instance, things like, I understood you were going to work on a book on Linda Kasabian, and you'd written a long piece on Haight-Ashbury and the Lucille Miller case, and all of the most painful things you could get your hands on, really.

JD: I'm not doing the book on Linda Kasabian now. I was working on one for a while. Well, there's certain things, I mean it's not consciously seeking things out but there's certain things that engage your imagination or don't, and sometimes something just sounds exactly . . .

SD: What you're looking for?

JD: What you want, well, not what you want, but what—this is something you have to do and I guess in that way it's an unconscious seeking out of . . .

SD: Your piece on the Haight was really—the thousands and thousands and probably millions of words that were written about that situation, yours seemed to me to get to the heart of it more than anything else, and yet you said that you felt—I think you said "frustrated" after it was published. That you were unhappy about it.

JD: Well, it was a very odd piece to do because I was there for quite a long time, longer than I'd ever spent before on a piece or after, and I kept staying because I kept having the sense that I wasn't getting it. I did not understand what was going on, and I finally came home, and I still didn't think I had it. I mean I still, you know, sometimes . . . Usually on a piece, there comes a day when you know you never have to do another interview. You can go home, you've gotten it. Well that day never came on that piece. The piece had to be written right away. So I wrote it right away. But I wrote it just in a series of scenes, exactly how it happened to me, and that was the only way that I could write it because I had no conclusions at all.

SD: But at the end of it did you still feel that you hadn't, even though it was highly praised and other people obviously thought that you had said something significant about the whole movement?

JD: That piece is a blank for me still. I have no idea whether it was good or bad.

SD: You zeroed in—as I notice you often do in other pieces—on the children as being, I mean I think there was three-year-old Michael, who lived in this kind of appalling barn thing and started a fire, and the little girl, Susan, who was on acid at five. Is that part of your being a mother, do you think?

JD: Well, that was very real to me then because I had a two-year-old at the time that I was working on that, and so it was particularly vivid to me to see these other children, and it was particularly vivid to me because I was away from the two-year-old, and feeling slightly . . .

SD: Cut off?
JD: Cut off from her, yeah.

SD: How much of your time, how much of your fears of living (if that's the expression), kind of zero in on Quintana, your own child?
JD: Well not a great deal. She's very—I mean I am apprehensive about everything and anxious, so I have to try to not lay this on her, and anyways she wouldn't have any of it if I did try.

SD: You described her at one point as being the kind of child that likes to get up in the morning.
JD: Oh yeah, she's very competent.

SD: Which brings me back to your own childhood and the piece you wrote in *Slouching Towards Bethlehem* about keeping a notebook. The way you told what to me seemed an incredible story about your mother giving you this notebook, and the first story you chose to note down in that was about the woman who thought she was freezing to death in Alaska or something and woke up to find that she was dying of heat in the Sahara. I think you were five, you said.
JD: Yeah.

SD: And I wondered what kind of sensibility in a child can possibly take that kind of a story and put it down as the first entry in her new notebook.
JD: Well, you know, I read someplace once that children, people in the nursery, within hours after birth, some children you can poke, the doctor can poke them and they don't flinch, and some children flinch. And then they've done studies about these children, and the children who flinch turn out to be flinchers all their life, and the others are extroverted or happy or competent children like my daughter. I think I was just a flincher at birth.

SD: You're not a subscriber to environment, obviously, because your own environment sounded very stable.

JD: Well, it was, it was very stable. My brother is an entirely different kind of person from me. It was mystifying to my mother and father, I think, why I was so despondent.

SD: Anaïs Nin, when she was here, talked a lot about the creative process in terms of neurosis, and the word *neurotic* was bandied about a lot. Do you think your anguish or your fears are realistic fears, or would you describe yourself as a neurotic?

JD: Well, at one point I would have described myself as a neurotic. I used to think of myself as a neurotic when I was in college. I think that was during a period when everybody was thinking of themselves as neurotic. I don't know now. I don't really think now in terms of neurosis. I think in terms of only extreme psychosis or normal. I mean or you're getting along all right. Someone asked me last night why I had never gone into analysis because I was so shy and I couldn't think what to say, and I said that finally I actually wouldn't want to go into analysis because if I found out too much about myself I might stop working, which is more important to me than being good at a dinner party.

SD: Anaïs wrote, "I care very much about the human condition but I will not die from caring." Do you think ever, you're in danger, you feel like dying metaphorically from caring too much and being unable to continue therefore?

JD: No, not at this point, no.

SD: Is it because you can put that caring into your work?

JD: Well, I think that everybody goes through a period of disgust—I don't mean disgust in terms of irritation but of kind of moral disgust with everybody else's—with the way the world is, and everything, and sometimes it seems pointless to write. But then you go through that to just working for yourself alone.

SD: But there are times for instance in the piece on Haight-Ashbury when you're feeling that everything is falling apart and that the center cannot hold. It's so intense that one wonders how on earth you could feel as intensely as that and still stay together, and still stay functioning.

JD: Well that's the trick. I mean, that's the way it's done. I mean, that was a period when I did feel that there was maybe not much point in writing, but, just my sheer interest in the techniques of writing kept me going, and also I needed money.

SD: The Linda Kasabian book is not coming out.
JD: No.

SD: What are you going to do next?
JD: Well, I'm starting another novel. And I'm starting a nonfiction book. I don't know which—I'll do one for a while and then pick up the other.

SD: Joan, thank you very much.

Notes

1. Sally Davis interviewed Anaïs Nin and Dory Previn along with Didion for this radio special.

A Day in the Life of Joan Didion

Susan Braudy / 1977

From *Ms.*, February 1977. © 1977 by Susan Braudy. Reprinted by permission.

I did not know why I did or did not do anything at all.
—Grace Mendana, in *A Book of Common Prayer*

Keepers of private notebooks are a different breed altogether, lonely and resistant rearrangers of things, anxious malcontents, children afflicted apparently at birth with some presentiment of loss.
—Joan Didion, on herself, in *Slouching Towards Bethlehem*

There hasn't been an American writer of Joan Didion's quality since Nathanael West.
—John Leonard, on *Play It As It Lays*

I am a Joan Didion fan. In her elegant and passionate essays written in the early sixties in such diverse publications as Vogue *and the* National Review, *and in the collection of essays,* Slouching Towards Bethlehem, *Didion focused on self-respect, morality, and the emotional empty places that lie beneath the most festooned surfaces of people. And in her first two novels,* Run River *(Ivan Obolensky),* Play It As It Lays *(Farrar, Straus & Giroux), she writes of women who are empty inside and who can't figure out how to cure their condition. Again, in the current and what is probably her finest novel,* A Book of Common Prayer *(Farrar, Straus & Giroux), her two women characters are depleted by the tragedies in their lives. The narrator Grace Mendana and her friend Charlotte Douglas are "norteamericanas" living in an imaginary equatorial republic, Boca Grande. Both are lost travelers, women who have lost a sense of purpose or destination to their lives.*

By writing this book about their life in Boca Grande, Grace, the book's narrator, is giving witness to her late friend Charlotte's life. Her witness is a new kind of prayer, an expression of love, for her friend's bleak and hopeless life. Like Camus's stranger, Meursault, Charlotte and Grace were not uncomfortable in the foreign Boca Grande because they have been "de afuera"—outsiders—all their lives.

Though she writes matter-of-factly that she is dying of cancer and that her house smells of it, Grace herself is a few steps closer to a kind of salvation than is Charlotte. It is in the act of writing the book that Grace affirms life.

Grace calls herself a lifetime student of delusion. She becomes fascinated with Charlotte's delusion and disintegration. Charlotte has led an unexamined life. She looks vague, seems to dream her life and is shocked at the age of 39 to discover that people die. As Grace describes Charlotte's privileged life, "Charlotte routinely asked [in her prayers,] that 'it' turn out all right, 'it' being unspecified and all-inclusive, and she had been an adult for some years before the possibility occurred to her that 'it' might not." Charlotte is also described by Grace's anthropologist self: "As a child of a comfortable family in the temperate zone she had been as a matter of course provided with clean sheets, orthodontia, lamb chops, living grandparents, attentive godparents, one brother named Dickie, ballet lessons, and casual timely information about menstruation and the care of fiat silver, as well as with a small wooden angel, carved in Austria, to sit on her bed table and listen to her prayers."

This new book is a dazzling example of Didion's themes. Her heroines always have the surfaces of their lives painted in perfect strokes. They have class, moneyed backgrounds, and lots of material things. They have at one time had, like Charlotte, dutiful husbands, expensive clothes, large well-run homes, strong appeal to the opposite sex, and nothing inside them but despair and confusion. Maria in Play It As It Lays *is a wanderer, a lost person, who rides the freeways aimlessly and tries to look decisive at the Coca-Cola machine for the benefit of the gasoline station attendants. Charlotte Douglas wanders aimlessly through the American South and then to Boca Grande. All these women have long forgotten why they are indifferent to or angry at their husbands and lovers, just as they've neglected to worry about having a career or a function. Most tragic for them, on Didion's terms, they have usually lost a child to mental deficiency or revolution or else been wounded by abortion.*

Didion's people seem almost heroic and purified by their suffering. Because she makes no comment on this, Didion has been accused by feminists of being masochistic, of believing that suffering is better than fighting back. She in turn has attacked several feminist books, in an article in the New York Times Book Review *a few years back, that I found almost impossible to understand.*

"Maybe," suggested a feminist editor, "she was saying that women are not a class worth defining, but she never really proved that. In fact she said they are more in touch with blood and life and death because they do menstruate and give birth."

"I never understood that piece too well," I answered. "But I think she was saying she's not a joiner, a political person, a utopist, that she's a loner, a Western writer, sort of a John Wayne character. She's against political cures for terror, loneliness, or pain. It's her art to describe the pain, not to cure it. And," I insisted, "I think she's the best woman writer in America right now who writes both fiction and nonfiction."

"Okay," said the editor, "but don't forget to ask her why she always writes about masochists, nonfunctioning women, when she herself is such a tough, highly functioning writer."

It is raining the morning I drive out to Malibu with a friend. On my left is the gray sea, luminescent like wrinkled silver foil. On my right are dirt-colored palisades, low cliffs covered by sparse bushes and straw-colored roots. Billboards tout fake Western restaurants and new motels and condominiums like the Esperanza with tennis, sauna, and Jacuzzi. Shacks and ugly little wooden motels block my view of the water on the left side of the road. As we drive north, the beach houses are more isolated and you can see more water. Then the houses are invisible behind fences and steep hills leading down to the sea. The land on the right looks jagged and falls into tiny valleys as though somebody cut it with a huge trowel. Rolling hills are covered with daisies, dune grass, and shrubs. Sandy mountains, blunted, uneven. We follow a trailer truck past Didion's steep road to her house, make a U-turn on the Pacific Coast highway and drive down to the sea.

"I'm Joan Dunne, come on in, come on in," she extends one long-fingered and skinny hand to shake. The blue cardigan sweater is slipping from her small shoulders, and she is pulling it back with one hand crossed over her chest. She is ducking her head uncertainly and not meeting my eyes. She finally stares for a second at the floor, her hair falling across her face. "Quintana Roo," she calls in a soft drawl, the word ending in a questioning noise. A robust California child, her daughter by adoption, strides into the room wearing a sweat shirt. She has a reddish-brown suntan, and sun-streaked blonde hair. She looks about ten. I am staring at Didion, at her pale skin, her light-blue eyeshadow, trying to memorize her physical appearance, while she looks pained as though she's sorry she's let somebody come into her house.

"It's awful to have rain," she apologizes as we walk to the tiled living room. The front of the house is all glass on the sea and sky. Didion sits with her back to the sea on an armchair. "My fantasy was that it would be sunny today and we would sit on the deck and eat chicken salad," she says with instant nostalgia. She bobs her head, and with the light from the gray sea and sky behind her, I have a hard time seeing her features, except for her eyes, too large for her face, and extending to the edges of it. She looks as though she has giant tear ducts. No matter if she is smiling, lighting a cigarette, or clutching a huge goblet filled with a Bloody Mary, she looks as though she could cry. She holds her chin high, and grips her body tight with her elbows, crosses her arms on her lap, fingers limp. Her hands shake both times she hands me a cup of coffee.

John Dunne comes in and sits in the other armchair. The two Dunnes chain-smoke and drink coffee, and the stream from the coffee and the smoke from their cigarettes curled up all afternoon against the sunless light that was the sea and the sky. The conversation turns at once to Hollywood. Dunne talks about the latest inside movie gossip.

The Dunnes are loath to discuss their screenplay for *A Star Is Born*. Later John Dunne will tell me, "Put it this way, it's our beads, but it's not our necklace." I watch them sitting in silence on matching beige easy chairs in their sparsely furnished living room with the terra-cotta tile floor. The ocean is the major furniture of the room. The horizon line appears and disappears. "I like the light," I tell her. "Yes." She leans forward so the light catches the reddish glint to her hair. "I love the light. It's like the ground absorbs it. I don't know. I think it's just . . ." and she raises her fingers toward her chest.

I compliment Didion on an article she wrote in the *New York Review of Books* in which she described how in Hollywood the deal is the art form. She says nothing. "Oh, my God, yes," her husband answers. "I think Joan's piece was the best thing ever written on the industry." I tell him I like his piece on screenwriting in the *Atlantic Monthly* and his excellent book called *Vegas: A Memoir of a Dark Season* (Random House). "It's fiction," Dunne says, "and the poems, you know, that were supposed to be written by that black prostitute Artha who worked the casinos, well, they were written by Joan."

"You see," Didion could be whispering, "John kept writing these poems that scanned and worked. He needed somebody to write some really bad poetry. I mean if you read those poems by Artha, there's always something a little wrong with them. They go lame in the last line."

Later I read one of the poems again in *Vegas*:

Star light,
Moon bright,
Will I save my life tonight?
In the stillness of the morn
The question is,
Why was I born?

I was at first surprised that John Dunne sat through most of the interview and did nearly all the talking. They are hard to talk to. They talk like the right and the left hands of a pianist.

JOAN DIDION: I don't hear the sound of the sea any more.

JOHN DUNNE: It's like the street sounds in New York. You filter them out.

JOAN: Usually you filter them out. When it's high tide or low tide, the waves actually stop. Then I wake up frightened in the middle of the night.

Joan disappears from time to time to get a new log for the fire. John disappears to answer the telephone. He reports that Katharine Ross just called. Friends say Joan rarely talks on the phone, that he handles this part of the outer world for her. I glance at the glass table next to the sofa; on it is a collection of seashells in a careful row next to photographs of John, Joan, and Quintana. A felt pen and a framed telex message are also lined up. The telex states that a certain number of Americans were killed in Vietnam on March 12, 1970.

I begin to lose track of who was telling me what. Joan and John don't interrupt each other in the flow of their conversation as much as they finish each other's paragraphs or repeat words they find needing in emphasis in the other's conversation. Their conversation is a two-person monologue.

JOHN: Did you see the SLA shootout on television? It was an apocalyptic event.

JOAN: The camera panned in and picked up a street sign.

JOHN: You could see the sun setting behind a palm tree.

JOAN: The house was on fire and then the palm tree caught fire.

JOHN: It was happening right in front of our eyes. Our telephone never stopped ringing.

JOAN: The palm tree was amazing. [She puts her arms together to make the trunk and spreads her fingers to be branches.]

JOHN: We were supposed to go out to dinner at seven-thirty. Everybody stayed home to watch the news.

JOAN: You know how dignified palm trees are. This had the outline of a palm tree, but it was a fireball. The camera just held on the palm tree and you could hear the . . .

JOHN: Crackling.

JOAN: Crackling. And you heard people saying, hey, you're in the line of fire.

JOHN: And here we were sitting on this placid ocean with the sun going down.

JOAN: You kept thinking you could be looking out the window and seeing it.

JOHN: Fire is so real here. In the fall you get the Santa Ana wind, and it whips through the canyon. It's so real to us. It's really scary, scary to see the flame.

JOAN: There was a fire up the highway. We were listening to the radio and we heard there was a roadblock on Oxnard, Route 39.

JOHN: Five miles are nothing if the wind is blowing. Fire will leap from a canyon. It can go five miles in five minutes because things are so dry.

JOAN: We had a map out but we couldn't find the fire.

JOHN: We had the bags packed and ready to go. All we had packed was Joan's manuscript and mine.

JOAN: And the silver.

JOHN: And the silver.

JOAN: After that we got a safe-deposit box. We got it for the manuscripts. But all we have in it is the pink slip for the Corvette and Quintana's birth certificate.

JOHN: But we got it for the manuscripts.

JOAN: Yes, but it takes organization to get things into it.

Only once during the breaks in mid-sentence did the Dunnes disagree. John announces that Viva had been taken on by Joan's literary agent and was the only person Joan ever sent her. "She's weird," John adds casually and smiles benignly. "No, she's not," Didion's elbows clutch her sides even tighter as she brings her long forefinger to her mouth. After a silence of about ten seconds, Dunne says, "No," and recrosses his legs. "Joan's right, she's not weird, well . . ." It was an awkward moment in an afternoon of trailing silences and pauses. Dunne made elisions, supplied topic sentences, ends of paragraphs and, after threatening silences, answered questions directed to Joan. The silence now about Viva was getting awkward. I had to speak; it took all my desire to see afternoons at the beach go well and not to stare at little children crying in restaurants. Their monologue was about to gain a third. "Everything Viva says *sounds* pretty reasonable," I offered.

Dunne leaves for a short time to drive to Xerox part of a novel he is writing, and Joan sits without him for ten minutes on some pillows on the floor beneath two huge photographs. One is of a desert road with mountains in the background and some signs. "Welcome to California" and "Death Valley."

It was while her husband was out that I asked Didion a question I had prepared in advance. If she was going to write a nonfiction piece about herself, what scene from her life would she lead with?

"Ah, I can't answer that question." She watches her hands as she smoothes her dungarees with her palms. "I mean it's ludicrous to be a thirty-nine-year-old woman who is shy, but I'm really too shy. I don't talk much. I am not articulate. I don't make judgments except when I'm sitting in front of the typewriter. I am a terrible interviewer. When I wrote about John Wayne, he kept sitting down and waiting for me to ask him questions. I had no questions."

A silence follows, and as the horizon line between the ocean and the gray sky disappears, I repeat my question. "No, no, I can't think of it. You know, sometimes I think I can't think at all unless I'm behind my typewriter. Like now I'm just recording sensory impressions, the light bouncing off the floor, your tapestry bag . . ."

Then Didion breaks yet another silence, "No, wait I do have a scene. I remember one day we had a bunch of people here for a beach party, and the house was filled with people. I began to feel scattered, upset, not myself. I could have gone and sat in the bathroom for a while by myself. I could have gone for a walk on the beach. Instead, I went to my office and just sat in front of my typewriter, and it was okay. I got control. I calmed down. I'm only myself in front of my typewriter."

Dunne returns and settles into this beige chair again. At a loss for something to say to start the conversation, I tell them that I find their house orderly. On the coffee table there is a tidy stack of books by people like Allen Tate and Robert Lowell.

John Dunne picks up the conversation smoothly. "Yes, orderly. We saw this house when it belonged to Michelle Phillips. The houses out here rent for thirty-five hundred a month in the summer, and we were living in a friend's house for the price of a mortgage. So since we fell in love with the area, we saw this place was for sale, and we called in a bid. In what was an indecently short time, they called us back to say it was ours. We knew we'd offered at least fifteen thousand too much."

Didion's rubber-soled shoes squinch on the tiles as she strides out for another log to heave onto the fire. "The place was a mess," she says.

"We walked in and thought what a mess," says Dunne, taking the log from her to throw it on the fire. "We said why did we buy it? The floors were covered with icky green wall-to-wall, and the walls were covered with plywood."

From the far corner of the room, Joan and Quintana are putting goblets and napkins on the table for lunch. Joan says, "You know that awful prefabricated plywood with fake wood marks and separations."

She disappears into the kitchen to return with limes and a cutting board. She slices the limes on the board on her lap, and then brings out some chicken. She shreds it with a knife into a bowl. In this pristine living room, the actions look elegant, like a holy ritual.

Dunne is talking about the house. "So we hired a contractor. Everyone who does that work out here once wrote a screenplay and is an actor. So we had to hear about everybody's problems—their work, their boyfriends, and their girlfriends—while they worked. We went East. We had paid them a lot of money to finish up, but it was like pouring money down a hole. The place was a mess when we got back.

"So we decided," and Dunne is still talking in his amiable cocktail party voice, "we should get a divorce. The house was killing us. When they brought in the jackhammer, Joan started crying in seconds. Quintana was screeching. So Joan hopped a plane and went home to Sacramento. I went to Las Vegas. But there was only a plastic sheet between us and the sea. The front wall had been torn out. We couldn't get a divorce. We couldn't sell the house." Now they both laugh, and we all walk to the table.

Sweet peas in a vase and a dish of eggs painted in watercolor are at the center. A helicopter in the sky appears to be flying lower than the house. During lunch Didion offers me her chicken salad garnished with lime juice and insists I take a painted egg and break its shell on my plate. She says, "If we didn't sell the house, we couldn't get a divorce, so we rehired the contractor and kept going. It was awful."

Their marriage has been a subject of some speculation ever since the late sixties when Didion launched her column for *Life* magazine. She wrote a piece in which she described herself as sitting by a pool in Hawaii and wondering if she should stay married. A recent *People* magazine article said that it is a rocky union. To me they seem a close team at this point. He seems more practical, the glue for their lives with his amiable and protective conversation.

After a while, I ask the feminist question. Why does she write about women in despair who believe in nothing and do nothing, when Didion herself is a strong woman who does a major thing—her writing? Why doesn't she write about women more like herself?

Didion is staring at her plate and picking at her egg. She looks like a kid eating quietly during a conversation by her elders. Dunne is speaking, "Whoever asks that question doesn't know a goddamn thing about the questions of literature. Joan writes because she writes."

Last winter, Didion went up to the University of California at Berkeley, where she'd been a student, to be a visiting regents lecturer. She spent a lot of time sitting alone in the faculty lounge and typing last-minute changes in her novel, *A Book of Common Prayer.* Her classroom, according to one student, was tense. She would either read aloud from a book like *The Education of Henry Adams* in her soft voice or she would drum her fingers on the desk in silence.

One evening she read a speech called "Why I Write" to faculty members. Before the speech she hid in the bathroom, convinced that she would vomit from nervous tension. After clearing her throat, she began with a sort of apology before she expressed her aesthetic. "I've been sitting here trying to get used to the idea that I'm here and you're there, but it may take me a little while. So if I look at my feet and don't talk very loud, I hope you'll bear with me until I get used to the idea."

Then her voice gets louder and begins to stress the consonants as she explains that she took the title "Why I Write" from an essay by George Orwell because she liked the sound of the words. "You have three short, unambiguous words that have the same sounds, and the sound they have is 'I, I, I.' In many ways writing is the act of saying 'I, I, I,' of imposing oneself upon other people—of saying 'listen to me, see it my way, change your mind.'"

The tremulous voice continues, "It's an aggressive act, sometimes a hostile act. You can disguise its aggressiveness all you want with veils of subordinate clauses and qualifiers and tentative subjunctive tenses and perhapses and elliptical treatments of things and evasions . . . But there's no getting around the fact that writing is an aggression. It's an imposition, it's an invasion of someone else's most private space . . ."

Didion goes on to say that she is not in the least bit intellectual, that she doesn't think in abstracts. "During the years I was an undergraduate at Berkeley, I tried. I kept trying to find that part of my mind that could deal in abstracts. But my mind kept veering inexorably back like some kind of boomerang I was stuck with—to the specific, to the tangible, to what was generally considered by everyone I knew, the peripheral. I would try to think about the Great Dialectic and I would find myself thinking instead about how the light was falling through the window in an apartment I had on the North Side. How it was hitting the floor."

Didion says that it took her years to find out what she was—a writer. "By which I mean not a good writer or a bad writer. . . . Obviously, I have to believe that some stuff I write is good or I wouldn't go on doing it. I couldn't get up in the morning.

"But I don't mean by a writer, a bad writer or a good writer. I just mean a person whose most absorbed and passionate hours are spent arranging words on pieces of paper. I get papers of different colors: yellow paper for getting it down, for notes, for letting it run; pale blue paper when I start getting closer to it, to find the shape of the thing—the grain in the wood. And I use white paper when it seems that if, if only I could commit myself to using this expensive paper, this sixteen-weight bond with a watermark on it, maybe if I make that commitment I could get it almost right. . . . I suppose if you get it entirely right, you may as well die or become a test pilot or move to Maryland or something."

She then discusses and discards Orwell's four motives for writing—egoism, historical enthusiasm, aesthetics, and to make a living. Of the last she says, "I do make a living writing, but I have never been convinced by anyone that there are not easier ways to make it. I think of alchemy as one."

At the core of her speech she says, "I write entirely to find out what is on my mind, what I'm thinking, what I'm looking at, what I'm seeing, and what it means. What I want and what I'm afraid of. . . . I'm not very interested in psychic cause and effect. In why I am the way I am and why you are the way you are."

Didion thought about her novel, *A Book of Common Prayer,* for six years and then wrote it in a year and a half. The book came out of a scene, a picture that she kept in her mind. It was of the Panama airport at six o'clock in the morning. She had stopped there for an hour on an Avianca plane that needed refueling on its way to Colombia.

"I can see that picture clearly," she told her audience at Berkeley. "We got off the plane. I can feel the tarmac under my feet. I can see the horizon. I can see the other plane. There was a Pan American plane sort of floating down at the end of the tarmac. Heat already rising off the tarmac at six o'clock in the morning. People inside playing slot machines. Very clear. The whole thing. And as a matter of fact, it's been superimposed on everything I've looked at for a couple of years now.

"Then I imagined I put a woman in the airport. The woman was in the coffee shop trying to get a cup of tea, but she insisted they boil the water for twenty minutes. What was that woman doing there? And I only had this. This hour in the Panama airport was my only experience in Central America."

When Didion talks about this picture, she defines it as having a "shimmer around the edges."

"There used to be an illustration in every beginning psychology textbook that showed a cat drawn by a patient in varying stages of schizophrenia. And the cat . . . well, it had a shimmer around it. . . . The cat became the background, the background became the cat. You could see they were interacting, exchanging ions. The whole molecular structure was breaking down around the edges of the cat.

"People on hallucinogenics describe the same perception of objects. I'm not a schizophrenic and I don't take hallucinogenics, but if you look hard enough you cannot miss that shimmer around the edges. . . . Writing is the attempt to understand what's going on in the shimmer. To find the cat in the shimmer, if the cat is the important thing, or to find what the shimmer is."

After Didion and her husband left that airport, she spent four days suffering from dysentery in a town on the Colombian coast. Out of these experiences, she began her book, some of which also takes place in San Francisco, and in the south of the United States.

Didion read a draft of the beginning of her novel aloud to her Berkeley audience. Then she said, "I mean, I don't really know. As I said, this appears to be a book about Charlotte. It may turn out to be about Grace. When I'm in the last twenty pages of it, I may have to go back through and pull—I may see it. I don't know, I have no idea. I still have not found the cat in the shimmer. And if I had found it, if I knew what this book was about, I wouldn't be writing it. That's why I write. Does anyone have any questions?"

A Visit with Joan Didion

Sara Davidson[1] / 1977

From *The New York Times Book Review,* April 3, 1977. © 1977 by Sara Davidson.
Reprinted by permission.

Her office is a chamber in which to dream waking dreams. There are props and cue cards. While she worked on *A Book of Common Prayer* a map of Central America hung on the wall. Set out on a table were postcards from Columbia, a newspaper photo of a janitor mopping up blood in a Caribbean hotel, books on tropical foliage and tropical medicine and a Viasa Airlines schedule with "Maracaibo-Paris" circled in blue. "Maracaibo-Paris—I thought those were probably the perimeters of the book," Joan Didion said.

I have been making the drive for six years and it never seems shorter: forty miles up the Pacific Coast Highway to Trancas, where Joan lives with her husband, John Gregory Dunne, and their daughter Quintana. Once past Malibu, the landscape changes. Wild mustard and cactus grow on the hills and the ocean front is no longer a protected bay, it is a seacoast.

I associate Joan Didion with the house in Trancas. The living room has a floor of large, square terra-cotta tiles, white brick walls, a redwood ceiling and a wall of glass doors looking out on the Pacific.

The props in the office have changed recently, as Joan prepares to start two new books, *Fairytales,* a non-fiction work about California, and *Angel Visits,* a novel set in Hawaii. "Joan never writes about a place that's not hot," John said. "The day she writes about a Boston winter will be a day it's all over."

On the Saturday in February when I drove out to interview Joan it was with some apprehension. She is not what one would call a virtuoso conversationalist. We taped four hours, of which Joan said later, "two hours were pauses." As I set up the machine, John Dunne wandered into the living room wearing a blue bathrobe. "I got the Saturday jits," he said. "I got anxiety crawling over me."

He asked Joan, "Do you have any Coke? Then I'll disappear, so I don't answer all your questions for you."

She brought him a Coca-Cola. He said, "Did you tell Sara the first line of *Angel Visits*?" She shook her head, no. He said the line from memory: "*I have never seen Madame Bovary in the flesh but imagine my mother dancing.*"

"Fantastic," I said. "Is there a comma after 'flesh'?"

Joan: "Yes."

John: "The first line, if you get it right, immediately sets the tone of the book."

Joan said, "It might change." After a pause, "I may take the comma out." (The next morning she indeed decided, "There shouldn't be a comma.")

When John had returned to his study, we settled on the couch. Joan was wearing a light-blue sweatshirt and faded, straight-leg jeans. Her reddish-blond hair was parted in the center and brushed behind her ears. She smoked Pall Malls or twisted a blue rubber band around her fingers, and at times her sentences trailed into a soft, rapid laughter.

Question: Could you talk about the origins of *A Book of Common Prayer*?

Answer: In the spring of '73, John and I went to Cartagena, Columbia, and the entire trip was like a hallucination, partly because I had a fever. It seemed to me extraordinary that North America had gone one way and South America had gone another, and I couldn't understand why. I kept reading that they had more resources than we had, they had more of everything and yet they had gone another way.

Question: How would you define the other way?

Answer: In North America, social tensions that arise tend to be undercut and co-opted quite soon, but in Latin America there does not seem to be any political machinery for delaying the revolution. Everything is thrown into bold relief. There is a collapsing of time. Everything is both older than you could ever know, and it started this morning.

Question: Did you read García Márquez's *One Hundred Years of Solitude*?

Answer: Yes, it's so wonderful. I was overcome by the book when I read it, but, when I went down there, I realized the book was far more social realism than it was fantasy. The element which had seemed to me fantastic was quite reportorial.

Question: Did you have a technical intention for this book?

Answer: Yes, I wrote it down on the map of Central America. "Surface like rainbow slick, shifting, fall, thrown away, iridescent." I wanted to do a deceptive surface that appeared to be one thing and turned color as you looked through it.

Question: What about the repetitions of phrases?
Answer: It seemed constantly necessary to remind the reader to make certain connections. Technically it's almost a chant. You could read it as an attempt to cast a spell or come to terms with certain contemporary demons. I can't think of what those demons are at the moment, but there's a range: flash politics, sexual adventurism.

Question: What has been your experience with politics?
Answer: I never had faith that the answers to human problems lay in anything that could be called political. I thought the answers, if there were answers, lay someplace in man's soul. I have an aversion to social action because it usually meant social regulation. It meant interference, rules, doing what other people wanted to do. The ethic I was raised in was specifically a Western frontier ethic. That means being left alone and leaving others alone. It is regarded by members of my family as the highest form of human endeavor.

Question: Do you vote?
Answer: Once in a while. I'm hardly ever conscious of issues. I mean they seem to me like ripples on an ocean. In the life of the body politic the actual movement is going on underneath, and I am interested in what's going on underneath. The politics I personally want are anarchic. Throw out the laws. Tear it down. Start all over. That is very romantic because it presumes that, left to their own devices, people would do good things for one another. I doubt that that's true. But I would like to believe it.

Question: Do you feel identified with Charlotte and Grace in this book?
Answer: I think you identify with all your characters. They become your family, closer to you than anybody you know. They kind of move into the house and take over the furniture. It's one of the difficult things about writing a book and leading a normal, social, domestic life.

Question: What is the effect of seeing people and getting a lot of stimulation?
Answer: It's quite destructive. Either you sit there and just close off or, if you do become engaged in what is going on with other people, then you have lost the thread. You've turned off the computer, and it is not for that period

of time making the connections it ought to be making. I really started thinking of my mind mechanically. I almost heard a steady humming if it was working all right, but if it stopped for a couple of days then it would take a while to get it back.

Question: In "Why I Write," there's a confidence expressed about the process of writing that I know you don't always feel.
Answer: I didn't express confidence so much as blind faith that if you go in and work every day it will get better. Three days will go by and you will be in that office and you will think every day is terrible. But on the fourth day, if you do go in, if you don't go into town or out in the garden, something usually will break through.

Question: How do you feel when you wake up?
Answer: Oh, I don't want to go in there at all. It's low dread, every morning. That dread goes away after you've been in there an hour. I keep saying "in there" as if it's some kind of chamber, a different atmosphere. It is, in a way. There's almost a psychic wall. The air changes. I mean you don't want to go through that door. But once you're in there, you're there, and it's hard to go out.

Question: I'd always assumed that, after you'd been writing for a number of years, that fear would disappear.
Answer: No, it doesn't. It's a fear you're not going to get it right. You're going to ruin it. You're going to fail. The touchy part on a book—when there's not the dread in the morning, when there's the dread all day long—is before it takes. Once it takes, there's just the morning dread and the occasional three days of terrible stuff; but before it takes, there's nothing to guarantee that it's going to take. There's a point in a novel where it shifts or the narrative won't carry. That point has to come before a third of the way through. It goes into overdrive. There are some novels you pick up and start reading and they're wonderful. Maybe you have to go to lunch or something and you get to page seventy and never pick them up again. You're not moved to keep turning pages. That's the narrative curve you've got to allow, around page seventy or eighty, to give it enough thrust to send it out. Imagine a rocket taking off. There's a point at which it drops its glitter or glamor and starts floating free.

Question: How do you feel about a book while you're writing it?
Answer: I try to hold my opinion in suspension. I hate the book when I'm working on it. But if I give way to that thought I would never finish the book, and then I would feel depressed and useless and have nothing to do all day.

Question: Have you ever not finished a book?
Answer: I've put things aside at forty pages.

Question: Did you get depressed?
Answer: Yes. There's a certain euphoric mania at first, when you think you've made the right decision and are really taking charge, but it sort of lies there as something you haven't finished. And you always wonder if maybe you had pushed a little harder it might have broken through. I mean it's a failure. So, starting anything, there's a great chance for psychic loss.

Question: How did you feel after finishing *A Book of Common Prayer*?
Answer: I was tired, so tired. I didn't want to read it. I haven't read it. I like it though, in an abstract way. It's like a dream again.

Question: I take it success and failure are important issues for you?
Answer: Yes, I suppose they are. I don't want to do anything that I don't do well. I don't want to ski. (*She laughs.*)

Question: What about tennis?
Answer: I do play tennis, not well, but I've moved into thinking of it as a way of getting color on my face and mild exercise, not as playing tennis. I haven't learned to serve yet. Every once in a while my teacher brings it up, but it takes too much coordination. He brought it up again last week, and I was on the verge of tears. I was furious, because I was really hitting the ball across the net pretty well.

Question: Could you talk about your writing method?
Answer: When I started this book, I wrote the first paragraph and continued for about three pages. Then I got scared and started skipping around and writing odd things.

Question: What did you get scared of?
Answer: Scared I couldn't sustain it. So I started writing odd bits here and there, and then I stopped being so scared when I had a pile of little things that appeared to be in the same tone as the beginning of the book. I just went back and started writing straight through until about page forty. By then the book was taking a slightly different direction. It was clear there was a narrator, for example. I had not intended there to be a narrator. I was going to be the female author's voice. I, the author, was going to tell you, the reader, the story. But the "I" became so strong that it became a character, so

I went back and rewrote those forty pages with that narrator. As the story developed, things kept changing; and you can push ahead for a little while knowing that those things are wrong back there, but you can't push too far or you lose precision. It doesn't matter to you as much, if you know it's wrong back there, so I started over again. I started over about twelve times. I wanted to start over when I went to Sacramento to finish it, but I didn't have time.

Question: You always go to Sacramento to finish your books. Is that a ritual?
Answer: It's very easy for me to work there. My concentration can be total because nobody calls me. I'm not required to lead a real life. I'm like a child, in my parents' house.

Question: Do you have a room there?
Answer: Yes. It's sort of a carnation-pink, and the vines and trees have grown up over the windows. It's exactly like a cave. It's a very safe place. It's a good room to work in; it's a finishing room. I once tried working in John's office here, and I was beside myself. There were too many books. I mean there was this weight of other people's opinions around me. I worked in the faculty club in Berkeley for a month, and it was very hard to work there because I didn't have the map of Central America. Not that Boca Grande is on the map, but the map took on a real life in my mind. I mean that very narrow isthmus. One of the things that worried me about this book was that there were several kinds of weather. It took place in San Francisco, the American South, and Central America. This sounds silly, but I was afraid that the narrative wouldn't carry if the weather changed. You wouldn't walk away from the book remembering one thing. The thing I wanted you to walk away remembering was the Central America weather. So all the things I had around my office had to do with Central America.

Question: Where did you get the title?
Answer: It just seemed right. *A Book of Common Prayer* was very important to this book. Why, I had no idea. At one point, my editor, Henry Robbins, asked what the title meant. I made up some specious thing and told him. I don't remember what I told him, something to the effect that the whole thing was a prayer. You could say that this was Grace's prayer for Charlotte's soul. If you have a narrator, which suddenly I was stuck with, the narrator

can't just be telling you a story, something that happened, to entertain you. The narrator has got to be telling you the story for a reason. I think the title probably helped me with that.

Question: Are you as skeptical about religion as you are about politics?
Answer: I am quite religious in a certain way. I was brought up Episcopalian, and I stopped going to church because I hated the stories. You know the story about the prodigal son? I have never understood that story. I have never understood why the prodigal son should be treated any better than the other son. I have missed the point of a lot of parables. But I like the words of the Episcopal service, and I say them over and over in my mind. There's one particular phrase which is part of every service: "As it was in the beginning, is now, and ever shall be, world without end. Amen." It's a very comforting phrase to a child. And to an adult. I have a very rigid sense of right and wrong. What I mean is, I use the words all the time. Even the smallest things. A table can be right or wrong.

Question: What about behavior?
Answer: Behavior is right or wrong. I was once having dinner with a psychiatrist who told me that I had monocular vision, and there was no need for everything to be right or wrong. Well, that way lies madness. In order to maintain a semblance of purposeful behavior on this earth you have to believe that things are right or wrong.

Question: What authors have influenced you?
Answer: As far as influence on style goes, I don't think you're influenced by anybody you read after age twenty. That all happens before you start working yourself. You would never know it from reading me, but I was very influenced by Hemingway when I was thirteen, fourteen, fifteen. I learned a lot about how sentences worked. How a short sentence worked in a paragraph, how a long sentence worked. Where the commas worked. How every word had to matter. It made me excited about words. Conrad, for the same reasons. The sentences sounded wonderful. I remember being so excited once, when I discovered that the key lines in *Heart of Darkness* were in parentheses. James, whom I didn't read until I was in college, was important to me in trying to come to terms with the impossibility of getting it right. James's sentences, with all those clauses, had to do with keeping the options open, letting the sentence cover as much as it could. That impressed me a great deal.

Question: What determines what you read now?
Answer: When I'm working I don't read much. If it's a good book it will depress me because mine isn't as good. If it's a bad book it will depress me because mine's just as bad. I don't want anybody else's speech rhythms in my dream. I never read *Ragtime*. I opened the first page and saw it had a very strong rhythm, so I just put it away like a snake.

Question: There's a certain aesthetic to the way you live. You once talked about using good silver every day.
Answer: Well, every day is all there is.

Question: Do you admire elegance?
Answer: Yes, because it makes you feel better. It's a form. I'm very attached to certain forms, little compulsive rituals. I like to cook; I like to sew. They're peaceful things, and they're an expression of caring.

Question: Could you talk about what you refer to as your shyness?
Answer: I like a lot of people, and I'm glad to see them, but I don't give the impression of being there. Part of it is that I'm terribly inarticulate. A sentence doesn't occur to me as a whole thing unless I'm working.

Question: Isn't it a surprise to people who read you and expect the same fluency in your conversation?
Answer: I don't know what they expect, but they certainly don't get it. (*Laughs.*) I don't know why, and I don't know what I can do about it, and it is easier for me to just write it off and try to do better at what I do well.

Question: Is John your editor?
Answer: Yes, we edit each other. A lot of people wonder how we can edit each other and live together, but it works out very well. We trust each other. Sometimes we don't agree. Obviously, you never want to agree when somebody tells you something doesn't work. I don't mean that kind of not agreeing. That's just when you're tired and it's midnight. I mean, sometimes, even on reflection, we don't agree, and there is a tacit understanding that neither of us will push too far. Each of us is aware that it would be easy to impose our sensibility, particularly our own style, on each other. And so there is a tacit agreement not to push beyond saying, "It doesn't work. This is how to fix it." If there is still a substantive disagreement, it's never mentioned again.

Question: Are you more interested in writing fiction these days than non-fiction?

Answer: I'm trying to do a non-fiction book now. I have always sort of wanted to write a book about California water. I'm interested in water—the pipes that water goes through, the mechanics of getting the water from place to place. I could look at a flume all day. I love dams, the way they are almost makes me weak, it's so beautiful.

Question: Are you intrigued with the movie community?

Answer: It interests me as an industry; you can watch it working. I like following the moves of the particular game. I like movie people. If I lived in Detroit, I would want to see automotive people. I would want to know what the moves were.

Question: Why do you write for movies?

Answer: One reason, obviously, is for the money. It's specious to say you could make the same amount of money writing a book. You can't write a book every year, but you have to keep on living every year. A lot of writers support themselves by teaching and lecturing. I don't like to do that. It uses up far more energy.

Question: What about the frustrations—deals falling through?

Answer: If your whole conception of yourself depended on whether or not you got a movie going, you might as well go up to San Francisco and get sad and jump. But ours doesn't. Our real life is someplace else. It's sort of a game. Also, it's very gratifying; it's fun, at least a first draft is fun. It's not like writing, it's like doing something else.

Question: Do you think it's proper or feasible to write about sex in an explicit way?

Answer: I don't think anything is improper in fiction, that there's any area that can't be dealt with. I don't in point of fact know very many people who deal with sex well. The only person who deals with sex in an explicit way whom I can read without being made profoundly uncomfortable is Norman Mailer. I know that's not an opinion shared by many. Mailer deals with sex in a very clean, direct way. There's no sentimentality around it. He takes it seriously. I tend to deal with sex obliquely. There is a lot of sexual content in *Common Prayer*, there was quite a lot in *Play It*

As It Lays too, but it was underneath. I'm just more comfortable dealing with it as an undertone.

Question: Some people complain that your female characters are passive drifters who lead purposeless lives. Do you see Charlotte Douglas that way?
Answer: No, I don't see that about any women I've written about. I think there is a confusion between passive and successful. Passive simply means passive, and active means active. Active doesn't necessarily imply success. Charlotte is very much in control there in Boca Grande when everyone else is running out.

Question: She doesn't seem to have a center, something in herself for which she's living.
Answer: Obviously the book finds her at a crisis. I don't know too many people who have what you could call clearly functioning centers.

Question: You have your work that sustains you no matter what. And devotion to your family.
Answer: They could all fall apart tomorrow. This is not a problem peculiar to women, it is a problem for all of us to find something at the center. Charlotte finds her center in Boca Grande. She finds her life by leaving it. I think most of us build elaborate structures to fend off spending much time in our own center.

Question: Do you think of yourself as sad or depressed?
Answer: No, I think of myself as really happy. Cheerful. I'm always amazed at what simple things can make me happy. I'm really happy every night when I walk past the windows and the evening star comes out. A star of course is not a simple thing, but it makes me happy. I look at it for a long time. I'm always happy, really.

Question: How do you feel about getting older?
Answer: I'm a very slow writer and I could count, if I wanted to—which I don't—the number of books I will have time to write. I work more. I work harder. There is a sense of urgency now.

Notes

1. Sara Davidson is the author of *Joan: Forty Years of Life, Loss, and Friendship with Joan Didion.* http://www.amazon.com/Joan-Forty-Years-Friendship-Didion-ebook/dp/B00LGJ7CPA/ref=sr_1_1?ie=UTF8&qid=1445886325&sr=8–1&keywords=Joan+didion+sara+davidson

Book of Common Prayer

Susan Stamberg / 1977

Susan Stamberg: "There are no terrific stories, there are only terrific ways of writing them down." Joan Didion said that, and proves it, in each of her novels: *Run River, Play It As It Lays*, and the newest, *A Book of Common Prayer*. They're depressing stories. Carefully, brilliantly sculpted, surgically written—about people to whom nothing makes any difference. Who move through bleached physical and emotional landscapes, creating a sense of imminent catastrophe.

Joan Didion is one of our very best writers. Forty-three years old, small, very thin—a Californian who doesn't look like a Californian, she says. She also says she writes entirely to find out what is on her mind—what she thinks, what she sees, what she's afraid of. She begins each book with a picture in her mind, and the act of writing is to find out what's going on in the picture. For *Run River*, the picture was of a house on a river in hot weather, a woman upstairs in the house, a man downstairs, and they weren't talking to one another. For *Play It As It Lays*, the picture was of a blond girl in a white halter dress being paged at one o'clock in the morning at a Las Vegas casino. For *A Book of Common Prayer*, the picture was of the Panama airport at six A.M., heat steaming up from the tarmac.

Joan Didion also writes nonfiction. A column, now, for *Esquire*. Earlier, journalism for *The Saturday Evening Post, The New York Times Magazine, Vogue*. Her best nonfiction essays are collected in the 1968 book *Slouching Towards Bethlehem*. Here's a quote from her introduction to that book: "My only advantage as a reporter is that I am so physically small, so temperamentally unobtrusive, and so neurotically inarticulate that people tend to forget that my presence runs counter to their best interests. And it always does. That is one last thing to remember: writers are always selling somebody out."

Joan Didion: That's an odd quote. People—when I go to colleges to talk—people are always asking me about "writers are always selling somebody out." And all I meant by it was that it is impossible to describe anybody—a friend, or somebody you know very well—and *please* them. Because your image of them, no matter how flattering, never corresponds with their self-image.

STAMBERG: It can be short or long?
DIDION: Right, yes.

STAMBERG: Now I hear it a different way for my work. I hear it as right now sitting here, wanting to talk to you about the things that most concern you in your life, and feeling I could never do that because there's no reason I should rip off *your* emotions and *your* privacy to make my living. That's how I hear this line.
DIDION: Really?

STAMBERG: Yes.
DIDION: I meant something so specific by it that it was . . .

STAMBERG: (*Interrupting*) But I'm saying the same thing you are, in a different way.
DIDION: Yes.

STAMBERG: You know, give me my great story. Tell me about your nervous breakdown, how awful it was. Give me my great radio tape. And knowing I could never dare, never dare to ask that. Or whatever. Because it simply would invade a kind of privacy that's nobody's damn business.
DIDION: I can never ask people even simple questions like—that all reporters know how to ask. I can never ask anybody how much money they made on something or . . . I think as a reporter I had to develop a stronger instinct for what was going on because I wasn't a very good reporter. I mean, I could never go out and get the story. And if I got into town where a story was and I found a *Life* team there I'd go home. I think a lot of the way people work comes out of their weaknesses, out of their failings.

STAMBERG: It's a way around something that other people can do straight on.

DIDION: If you can't talk to the mayor, then maybe if you sit around the gas station and figure out what it's all about, it will . . . I almost use interviews, when I do do them in that kind of situation, as just a way of insinuating myself into the person's day. That the actual answers aren't ever very significant. I'm never happier than if I go on a story and I find myself with the person and they're doing whatever they do and it turns out, maybe—let's just say it's on a movie set—and it turns out that they're too busy to give me twenty minutes, because I am there without having to go through the interview. (*laughter*)

STAMBERG: Yes. That desolate landscape that you create, and those characters who move through it in their parched ways—it seems to me you're giving kind of a worldview in that, and it also seems to me that you'd never get a Nobel Prize for Literature. Not because of any lack of *skill*, mind you, but because that prize is given for optimistic and positive views of life.

DIDION: I am more attracted to the underside of the tapestry. I tend to always look for the wrong side, the bleak side. I have since I was a child. I have no idea why. I'm rather a slow study, and I came late to the apprehension that there was a void at the center of experience. A lot of people realize this when they're fifteen or sixteen, but I didn't realize it until I was writing *Play It As It Lays.* And until around that time . . . that it was possible that the dark night of the soul was . . . it had not occurred to me that it was dryness, that it was aridity. I had thought that it was something much riper and sinful. And I think that *Play It As It Lays* was a way of working that out, dealing myself with the idea that experience was largely meaningless. It seems to me my adult life has been a succession of expectations, misperceptions, that I dealt only with an idea I had of the world, not with the world as it was. Reality *does* intervene. One of the books that made the strongest impression on me when I was in college, I remember, was *The Portrait of a Lady.* Isabel Archer was the prototype romantic idealist. And it trapped her, and she ended up a prisoner of her own idea. And I think a lot of us do.

STAMBERG: You talk a lot about the picture that's in your mind. And that picture [of] the tarmac in Boca Grande—in Panama, actually—which was with you, you lived with it for several years. You finished that book. Do you have a picture in your mind, now, of something else that you're going to have to be working on?

DIDION: Yes. My next novel is going to take place in Hawaii. I can't describe the picture, except that it is very pink and it smells like flowers, and I'm afraid to describe it out loud because if I describe it out loud I won't write it down.

STAMBERG: Joan Didion. Her new novel is *A Book Of Common Prayer.* Her next novel hasn't begun to be written, and she doesn't really know what it will be about beyond that pink and fragrant picture. Joan Didion says if she did know what it was about, she wouldn't need to write it.

Joan Didion: The Art of Fiction No. 71

Linda Kuehl / 1978

From *The Paris Review*, Issue 74, Fall-Winter 1978. Copyright © 1978 by The Paris Review. Reprinted by permission of the Wylie Agency LLC.

It is usual for the interviewer to write this paragraph about the circumstances in which the interview was conducted, but the interviewer in this case, Linda Kuehl, died not long after the tapes were transcribed. Linda and I talked on August 18 and August 24, 1977, from about ten in the morning until early afternoon. Both interviews took place in the living room of my husband's and my house on the ocean north of Los Angeles, a house we no longer own. The walls in that room were white. The floors were of terracotta tile, very highly polished. The glare off the sea was so pronounced in that room that corners of it seemed, by contrast, extremely dark, and everyone who sat in the room tended to gravitate toward these dark corners. Over the years the room had in fact evolved to the point where the only comfortable chairs were in the dark, away from the windows. I mention this because I remember my fears about being interviewed, one of which was that I would be construed as the kind of loon who had maybe three hundred degrees of sea view and kept all the chairs in a kind of sooty nook behind the fireplace. Linda's intelligence dispelled these fears immediately. Her interest in and acuity about the technical act of writing made me relaxed and even enthusiastic about talking, which I rarely am. As a matter of fact, this enthusiasm for talking technically makes me seem to myself, as I read over the transcript, a kind of apprentice plumber of fiction, a Cluny Brown at the writer's trade, but there we were.

INTERVIEWER: You have said that writing is a hostile act; I have always wanted to ask you why.

JOAN DIDION: It's hostile in that you're trying to make somebody see something the way you see it, trying to impose your idea, your picture. It's hostile to try to wrench around someone else's mind that way. Quite often you want to tell somebody your dream, your nightmare. Well, nobody wants to hear about someone else's dream, good or bad; nobody wants to walk around with it. The writer is always tricking the reader into listening to the dream.

INTERVIEWER: Are you conscious of the reader as you write? Do you write listening to the reader listening to you?

DIDION: Obviously I listen to a reader, but the only reader I hear is me. I am always writing to myself. So very possibly I'm committing an aggressive and hostile act toward myself.

INTERVIEWER: So when you ask, as you do in many nonfiction pieces, "Do you get the point?" you are really asking if you *yourself* get the point.

DIDION: Yes. Once in a while, when I first started to write pieces, I would try to write to a reader other than myself. I always failed. I would freeze up.

INTERVIEWER: When did you know you wanted to write?

DIDION: I wrote stories from the time I was a little girl, but I didn't want to be a writer. I wanted to be an actress. I didn't realize then that it's the same impulse. It's make-believe. It's performance. The only difference being that a writer can do it all alone. I was struck a few years ago when a friend of ours—an actress—was having dinner here with us and a couple of other writers. It suddenly occurred to me that she was the only person in the room who couldn't plan what she was going to do. She had to wait for someone to ask her, which is a strange way to live.

INTERVIEWER: Did you ever have a writing teacher?

DIDION: Mark Schorer was teaching at Berkeley when I was an undergraduate there, and he helped me. I don't mean he helped me with sentences, or paragraphs—nobody has time for that with student papers; I mean that he gave me a sense of what writing was about, what it was for.

INTERVIEWER: Did any writer influence you more than others?

DIDION: I always say Hemingway, because he taught me how sentences worked. When I was fifteen or sixteen I would type out his stories to learn how the sentences worked. I taught myself to type at the same time. A few years ago when I was teaching a course at Berkeley I reread *A Farewell to Arms* and fell right back into those sentences. I mean, they're perfect sentences. Very direct sentences, smooth rivers, clear water over granite, no sinkholes.

INTERVIEWER: You've called Henry James an influence.

DIDION: He wrote perfect sentences, too, but very indirect, very complicated. Sentences *with* sinkholes. You could drown in them. I wouldn't dare to write one. I'm not even sure I'd dare to read James again. I loved those novels so much that I was paralyzed by them for a long time. All those possibilities. All that perfectly reconciled style. It made me afraid to put words down.

INTERVIEWER: I wonder if some of your nonfiction pieces aren't shaped as a single Jamesian sentence.

DIDION: That would be the ideal, wouldn't it. An entire piece—eight, ten, twenty pages—strung on a single sentence. Actually, the sentences in my nonfiction are far more complicated than the sentences in my fiction. More clauses. More semicolons. I don't seem to hear that many clauses when I'm writing a novel.

INTERVIEWER: You have said that once you have your first sentence you've got your piece. That's what Hemingway said. All he needed was his first sentence and he had his short story.

DIDION: What's so hard about that first sentence is that you're stuck with it. Everything else is going to flow out of that sentence. And by the time you've laid down the first *two* sentences, your options are all gone.

INTERVIEWER: The first is the gesture, the second is the commitment.

DIDION: Yes, and the last sentence in a piece is another adventure. It should open the piece up. It should make you go back and start reading from page one. That's how it *should* be, but it doesn't always work. I think of writing anything at all as a kind of high-wire act. The minute you start putting words on paper you're eliminating possibilities. Unless you're Henry James.

INTERVIEWER: I wonder if your ethic—what you call your "harsh Protestant ethic"—doesn't close things up for you, doesn't hinder your struggle to keep all the possibilities open.

DIDION: I suppose that's part of the dynamic. I start a book and I want to make it perfect, want it to turn every color, want it to *be the world*. Ten pages in, I've already blown it, limited it, made it less, marred it. That's very discouraging. I hate the book at that point. After a while I arrive at an accommodation: Well, it's not the ideal, it's not the perfect object I wanted to make, but maybe—if I go ahead and finish it anyway—I can get it right next time. Maybe I can have another chance.

INTERVIEWER: Have any women writers been strong influences?

DIDION: I think only in the sense of being models for a life, not for a style. I think that the Brontës probably encouraged my own delusions of theatricality. Something about George Eliot attracted me a great deal. I think I was not temperamentally attuned to either Jane Austen or Virginia Woolf.

INTERVIEWER: What are the disadvantages, if any, of being a woman writer?

DIDION: When I was starting to write—in the late fifties, early sixties—there was a kind of social tradition in which male novelists could operate. Hard drinkers, bad livers. Wives, wars, big fish, Africa, Paris, no second acts. A man who wrote novels had a role in the world, and he could play that role and do whatever he wanted behind it. A woman who wrote novels had no particular role. Women who wrote novels were quite often perceived as invalids. Carson McCullers, Jane Bowles. Flannery O'Connor, of course. Novels by women tended to be described, even by their publishers, as sensitive. I'm not sure this is so true anymore, but it certainly was at the time, and I didn't much like it. I dealt with it the same way I deal with everything. I just tended my own garden, didn't pay much attention, behaved—I suppose—deviously. I mean I didn't actually let too many people know what I was doing.

INTERVIEWER: Advantages?

DIDION: The advantages would probably be precisely the same as the disadvantages. A certain amount of resistance is good for anybody. It keeps you awake.

INTERVIEWER: Can you tell simply from the style of writing, or the sensibility, if the author is a woman?

DIDION: Well, if style is character—and I believe it is—then obviously your sexual identity is going to show up in your style. I don't want to differentiate between style and sensibility, by the way. Again, your style *is* your sensibility. But this whole question of sexual identity is very tricky. If I were to read, cold, something by Anaïs Nin, I would probably say that it was written by a man trying to write as a woman. I feel the same way about Colette, and yet both those women are generally regarded as intensely "feminine" writers.

I don't seem to recognize "feminine." On the other hand, *Victory* seems to me a profoundly female novel. So does *Nostromo,* so does *The Secret Agent.*

INTERVIEWER: Do you find it easy to write in depth about the opposite sex?

DIDION: *Run River* was partly from a man's point of view. Everett McClellan. I don't remember those parts as being any harder than the other parts. A lot of people thought Everett was "shadowy," though. He's the most distinct person in the book to me. I loved him. I loved Lily and Martha, but I loved Everett more.

INTERVIEWER: Was *Run River* your first novel? It seems so finished for a first that I thought you might have shelved earlier ones.

DIDION: I've put away nonfiction things, but I've never put away a novel. I might throw out forty pages and write forty new ones, but it's all part of the same novel. I wrote the first half of *Run River* at night over a period of years. I was working at *Vogue* during the day, and at night I would work on these scenes for a novel. In no particular sequence. When I finished a scene I would tape the pages together and pin the long strips of pages on the wall of my apartment. Maybe I wouldn't touch it for a month or two, then I'd pick a scene off the wall and rewrite it. When I had about a hundred and fifty pages done I showed them to twelve publishers, all of whom passed. The thirteenth, Ivan Obolensky, gave me an advance, and with that thousand dollars or whatever it was I took a two-month leave of absence and wrote the last half of the book. That's why the last half is better than the first half. I kept trying to run the first half through again, but it was intractable. It was set. I'd worked on it for too many years in too many moods. Not that the last half is perfect. It's smoother, it moves faster, but there are a great many unresolved problems. I didn't know how to do anything at all. I had wanted *Run River* to be very complicated chronologically, to somehow have the past and present operating simultaneously, but I wasn't accomplished enough to do that with any clarity. Everybody who read it said it wasn't working. So I straightened it out. Present time to flashback to present time. Very straight. I had no option, because I didn't know how to do it the other way. I just wasn't good enough.

INTERVIEWER: Did you or Jonathan Cape put the comma in the title of the English edition?

DIDION: It comes back to me that Cape put the comma in and Obolensky left the comma out, but it wasn't of very much interest to me because I hated it both ways. The working title was *In the Night Season,* which Obolensky didn't like. Actually, the working title during the first half was

Harvest Home, which everybody dismissed out of hand as uncommercial, although later there was a big commercial book by Thomas Tyron called exactly that. Again, I was not very sure of myself then, or I never would have changed the title.

INTERVIEWER: Was the book autobiographical? I ask this for the obvious reason that first novels often are.

DIDION: It wasn't except that it took place in Sacramento. A lot of people there seemed to think that I had somehow maligned them and their families, but it was just a made-up story. The central incident came from a little one-inch story in *The New York Times* about a trial in the Carolinas. Someone was on trial for killing the foreman on his farm, that's all there was. I think I really put the novel in Sacramento because I was homesick. I wanted to remember the weather and the rivers.

INTERVIEWER: The heat on the rivers?

DIDION: The heat. I think that's the way the whole thing began. There's a lot of landscape that I never would have described if I hadn't been homesick. If I hadn't wanted to remember. The impulse was nostalgia. It's not an uncommon impulse among writers. I noticed it when I was reading *From Here to Eternity* in Honolulu just after James Jones died. I could see exactly that kind of nostalgia, that yearning for a place, overriding all narrative considerations. The incredible amount of description. When Prewitt tries to get from the part of town where he's been wounded out to Alma's house, every street is named. Every street is described. You could take that passage and draw a map of Honolulu. None of those descriptions have any narrative meaning. They're just remembering. Obsessive remembering. I could see the impulse.

INTERVIEWER: But doesn't the impulse of nostalgia produce the eloquence in *Run River?*

DIDION: It's got a lot of sloppy stuff. Extraneous stuff. Words that don't work. Awkwardness. Scenes that should have been brought up, scenes that should have been played down. But then *Play It As It Lays* has a lot of sloppy stuff. I haven't reread *Common Prayer,* but I'm sure that does, too.

INTERVIEWER: How did you come to terms with point of view in *Play It As It Lays?* Did you ever question your authority to do it in both first and third person?

DIDION: I wanted to make it all first person, but I wasn't good enough to maintain at first. There were tricks I didn't know. So I began playing with a close third person, just to get something down. By a "close third" I mean not an omniscient third but a third very close to the mind of the character. Suddenly one night I realized that I had some first person and some third person and that I was going to have to go with both, or just not write a book at all. I was scared. Actually, I don't mind the way it worked out. The juxtaposition of first and third turned out to be very useful toward the ending, when I wanted to accelerate the whole thing. I don't think I'd do it again, but it was a solution to that particular set of problems. There's a point when you go with what you've got. Or you don't go.

INTERVIEWER: How long, in all, did *Play It As It Lays* take to write?
DIDION: I made notes and wrote pages over several years, but the actual physical writing—sitting down at the typewriter and working every day until it was finished—took me from January until November 1969. Then of course I had to run it through again—I never know quite what I'm doing when I'm writing a novel, and the actual line of it doesn't emerge until I'm finishing. Before I ran it through again I showed it to John and then I sent it to Henry Robbins, who was my editor then at Farrar, Straus. It was quite rough, with places marked "chapter to come." Henry was unalarmed by my working that way, and he and John and I sat down one night in New York and talked, for about an hour before dinner, about what it needed doing. We all knew what it needed. We all agreed. After that I took a couple of weeks and ran it through. It was just typing and pulling the line through.

INTERVIEWER: What do you mean exactly by "pulling through"?
DIDION: For example, I didn't know that BZ was an important character in *Play It As It Lays* until the last few weeks I was working on it. So those places I marked "chapter to come" were largely places where I was going to go back and pull BZ through, hit him harder, prepare for the way it finally went.

INTERVIEWER: How did you feel about BZ's suicide at the end?
DIDION: I didn't realize until after I'd written it that it was essentially the same ending as *Run River*. The women let the men commit suicide.

INTERVIEWER: I read that *Play It As It Lays* crystallized for you when you were sitting in the lobby of the Riviera Hotel in Las Vegas and saw a girl walk through.
DIDION: I had thought Maria lived in New York. Maybe she was a model. Anyway, she was getting a divorce, going through grief. When I

saw this actress in the Riviera Hotel, it occurred to me that Maria could be an actress. In California.

INTERVIEWER: Was she always Maria Wyeth?

DIDION: She didn't even have a name. Sometimes I'll be fifty, sixty pages into something and I'll still be calling a character "X." I don't have a very clear idea of who the characters are until they start talking. Then I start to love them. By the time I finish the book, I love them so much that I want to stay with them. I don't want to leave them ever.

INTERVIEWER: Do your characters talk to you?

DIDION: After a while. In a way. When I started *Common Prayer*, all I knew about Charlotte was that she was a nervous talker and told pointless stories. A distracted kind of voice. Then one day I was writing the Christmas party at the American embassy, and I had Charlotte telling these bizarre anecdotes with no point while Victor Strasser-Mendana keeps trying to find out who she is, what she's doing in Boca Grande, who her husband is, what her husband does. And suddenly Charlotte says, "He runs guns. I wish they had caviar." Well, when I heard Charlotte say this, I had a very clear fix on who she was. I went back and rewrote some early stuff.

INTERVIEWER: Did you reshuffle a lot and, if so, how? Did you use pins or tape or what?

DIDION: Toward the beginning of a novel I'll write a lot of sections that lead me nowhere. So I'll abandon them, pin them on a board with the idea of picking them up later. Quite early in *Common Prayer* I wrote a part about Charlotte Douglas going to airports, a couple of pages that I liked but couldn't seem to find a place for. I kept picking this part up and putting it in different places, but it kept stopping the narrative; it was wrong everywhere, but I was determined to use it. Finally I think I put it in the middle of the book. Sometimes you can get away with things in the middle of a book. The first hundred pages are very tricky, the first forty pages especially. You have to make sure you have the characters you want. That's really the most complicated part.

INTERVIEWER: Strategy would seem to be far more complicated in *Common Prayer* than in *Play It As It Lays* because it had so much more plot.

DIDION: *Common Prayer* had a lot of plot and an awful lot of places and weather. I wanted a dense texture, and so I kept throwing stuff into it, making promises. For example, I promised a revolution. Finally, when I got within twenty pages of the end, I realized I still hadn't delivered this revolution. I had a lot of threads, and I'd overlooked this one. So then I had to go back and lay in the preparation for the revolution. Putting in that revolution was like setting in a sleeve. Do you know what I mean? Do you sew? I mean I had to work that revolution in on the bias, had to ease out the wrinkles with my fingers.

INTERVIEWER: So the process of writing the novel is for you the process of discovering the precise novel that you want to write.
DIDION: Exactly. At the beginning I don't have anything at all, don't have any people, any weather, any story. All I have is a technical sense of what I want to do. For example, I want sometime to write a very long novel, eight hundred pages. I want to write an eight-hundred-page novel precisely *because* I think a novel should be read at one sitting. If you read a novel over a period of days or weeks the threads get lost, the suspension breaks. So the problem is to write an eight-hundred-page novel in which all the filaments are so strong that nothing breaks or gets forgotten ever. I wonder if García Márquez didn't do that in *The Autumn of the Patriarch.* I don't want to read it because I'm afraid he might have done it, but I did look at it, and it seems to be written in a single paragraph. *One paragraph.* The whole novel. I love that idea.

INTERVIEWER: Do you have any writing rituals?
DIDION: The most important is that I need an hour alone before dinner, with a drink, to go over what I've done that day. I can't do it late in the afternoon because I'm too close to it. Also, the drink helps. It removes me from the pages. So I spend this hour taking things out and putting other things in. Then I start the next day by redoing all of what I did the day before, following these evening notes. When I'm really working I don't like to go out or have anybody to dinner, because then I lose the hour. If I don't have the hour, and start the next day with just some bad pages and nowhere to go, I'm in low spirits. Another thing I need to do, when I'm near the end of the book, is sleep in the same room with it. That's one reason I go home to Sacramento to finish things. Somehow the book doesn't leave you when you're asleep right next to it. In Sacramento nobody cares if I appear or not. I can just get up and start typing.

INTERVIEWER: What's the main difference between the process of fiction and the process of nonfiction?

DIDION: The element of discovery takes place, in nonfiction, not during the writing but during the research. This makes writing a piece very tedious. You already know what it's about.

INTERVIEWER: Are the subject of pieces determined by editors or are you free to go your own way?

DIDION: I make them up. They reflect what I want to do at the time, where I want to be. When I worked for *Life* I did a great many Honolulu pieces— probably more than *Life* might have wanted—because that's where I wanted to be then. Last night I finished a piece for *Esquire* about the California Water Project. I had always wanted to see the room where they control the water, where they turn it on and off all over the state, and I also wanted to see my mother and father. The water and my mother and father were all in Sacramento, so I went to Sacramento. I like to do pieces because it forces me to make appointments and see people, but I never wanted to be a journalist or reporter. If I were doing a story and it turned into a big breaking story, all kinds of teams flying in from papers and magazines and the networks, I'd probably think of something else to do.

INTERVIEWER: You've said that when you were an editor at *Vogue*, Allene Talmey showed you how verbs worked.

DIDION: Every day I would go into her office with eight lines of copy or a caption or something. She would sit there and mark it up with a pencil and get very angry about extra words, about verbs not working. Nobody has time to do that except on a magazine like *Vogue*. Nobody, no teacher. I've taught and I've tried to do it, but I didn't have that much time and neither did the students. In an eight-line caption everything had to work, every word, every comma. It would end up being a *Vogue* caption, but on its own terms it had to work perfectly.

INTERVIEWER: You say you treasure privacy, that "being left alone and leaving others alone is regarded by members of my family as the highest form of human endeavor." How does this mesh with writing personal essays, particularly the first column you did for *Life* where you felt it imperative to inform the reader that you were at the Royal Hawaiian Hotel in lieu of getting a divorce?

DIDION: I don't know. I could say that I was writing to myself, and of course I was, but it's a little more complicated than that. I mean the fact that eleven million people were going to see that page didn't exactly escape my attention. There's a lot of mystery to me about writing and performing and showing off in general. I know a singer who throws up every time she has to go onstage. But she still goes on.

INTERVIEWER: How did the "fragility of Joan Didion" myth start?

DIDION: Because I'm small, I suppose, and because I don't talk a great deal to people I don't know. Most of my sentences drift off, don't end. It's a habit I've fallen into. I don't deal well with people. I would think that this appearance of not being very much in touch was probably one of the reasons I started writing.

INTERVIEWER: Do you think some reviewers and readers have mistaken you for your characters?

DIDION: There was a certain tendency to read *Play It As It Lays* as an autobiographical novel, I suppose because I lived out here and looked skinny in photographs and nobody knew anything else about me. Actually, the only thing Maria and I have in common is an occasional inflection, which I picked up from her—not vice versa—when I was writing the book. I like Maria a lot. Maria was very strong, very tough.

INTERVIEWER: That's where I have difficulty with what so many critics have said about your women. Your women hardly seem fragile to me.

DIDION: Did you read Diane Johnson's review of *Common Prayer* in *The New York Review of Books*? She suggested that the women were strong to the point of being figures in a romance, that they were romantic heroines rather than actual women in actual situations. I think that's probably true. I think I write romances.

INTERVIEWER: I'd like to ask you about things that recur in your work. There's the line about "dirty tulips" on Park Avenue in a short story and in a piece. Or how about the large, square emerald ring that Lily wears in *Run River* and Charlotte wears in *Common Prayer*?

DIDION: Does Lily wear one, too? Maybe she does. I've always wanted one, but I'd never buy one. For one thing emeralds—when you look at them closely—are always disappointing. The green is never blue enough. Ideally, if the green were blue enough you could look into an emerald for the rest of your life. Sometimes I think about Katherine Anne Porter's emeralds, sometimes I wonder if they're blue enough. I hadn't planned that emerald in *Common Prayer* to recur the way it does. It was just something I thought

Charlotte might have, but as I went along the emerald got very useful. I kept taking that emerald one step further. By the end of the novel the emerald is almost the narrative. I had a good time with that emerald.

INTERVIEWER: What about the death of a parent, which seems to recur as a motif?

DIDION: You know how doctors who work with children get the children to tell stories? And they figure out from the stories what's frightening the child, what's worrying the child, what the child thinks? Well, a novel is just a story. You work things out in the stories you tell.

INTERVIEWER: And the abortion or loss of a child?

DIDION: The death of children worries me all the time. It's on my mind. Even *I* know that, and I usually don't know what's on my mind. On the whole, I don't want to think too much about why I write what I write. If I know what I'm doing I don't do it, I can't do it. The abortion in *Play It As It Lays* didn't occur to me until I'd written quite a bit of the book. The book needed an active moment, a moment at which things changed for Maria, a moment in which—this was very, very important—Maria was center stage for a number of pages. Not at a party reacting to somebody else. Not just thinking about her lot in life, either. A long section in which she was the main player. The abortion was a narrative strategy.

INTERVIEWER: Was it a narrative strategy in *Run River?*

DIDION: Actually, it was the excuse for a digression, into landscape. Lily has an abortion in San Francisco and then she comes home on the Greyhound bus. I always think of the Greyhound bus and not the abortion. The bus part is very detailed about the look of the towns. It's something I wrote in New York; you can tell I was homesick.

INTERVIEWER: How about the freeways that reappear?

DIDION: Actually, I don't drive on the freeway. I'm afraid to. I freeze at the top of the entrance, at the instant when you have to let go and join it. Occasionally I *do* get on the freeway—usually because I'm shamed into it—and it's such an extraordinary experience that it sticks in my mind. So I use it.

INTERVIEWER: And the white space at the corner of Sunset and La Brea in Hollywood? You mention it in some piece and then in *Play It As It Lays.*

DIDION: I've never analyzed it, but one line of poetry I always have in mind is the line from *Four Quartets*: "at the still point of the turning world." I tend to move toward still points. I think of the equator as a still point. I suppose that's why I put Boca Grande on the equator.

INTERVIEWER: A narrative strategy.

DIDION: Well, this whole question of how you work out the narrative is very mysterious. It's a good deal more arbitrary than most people who don't do it would ever believe. When I started *Play It As It Lays* I gave Maria a child, a daughter, Kate, who was in kindergarten. I remember writing a passage in which Kate came home from school and showed Maria a lot of drawings, orange and blue crayon drawings, and when Maria asked her what they were, Kate said, "Pools on fire." You can see I wasn't having too much success writing this child. So I put her in a hospital. You never meet her. Now, it turned out to have a great deal of importance—Kate's being in the hospital is a very large element in *Play It As It Lays*—but it began because I couldn't write a child, no other reason. Again, in *Common Prayer,* Marin bombs the Transamerica Building because I *needed* her to. I needed a crisis in Charlotte's life. Well, at this very moment, right now, I can't think of the Transamerica Building without thinking of Marin and her pipe bomb and her gold bracelet, but it was all very arbitrary in the beginning.

INTERVIEWER: What misapprehensions, illusions and so forth have you had to struggle against in your life? In a commencement address you once said there were many.

DIDION: All kinds. I was one of those children who tended to perceive the world in terms of things read about it. I began with a literary idea of experience, and I still don't know where all the lies are. For example, it may not be true that people who try to fly always burst into flames and fall. That may not be true at all. In fact people *do fly,* and land safely. But I don't really believe that. I still see Icarus. I don't seem to have a set of physical facts at my disposal, don't seem to understand how things really work. I just have an *idea* of how they work, which is always trouble. As Henry James told us.

INTERVIEWER: You seem to live your life on the edge, or, at least, on the literary idea of the edge.

DIDION: Again, it's a literary idea, and it derives from what engaged me imaginatively as a child. I can recall disapproving of the golden mean, always thinking there was more to be learned from the dark journey. The dark journey engaged me more. I once had in mind a very light novel, all surface, all conversations and memories and recollections of some people in Honolulu who were getting along fine, one or two misapprehensions about the past notwithstanding. Well, I'm working on that book now, but it's not running that way at all. Not at all.

INTERVIEWER: It always turns into danger and apocalypse.

DIDION: Well, I grew up in a dangerous landscape. I think people are more affected than they know by landscapes and weather. Sacramento was a very extreme place. It was very flat, flatter than most people can imagine, and I still favor flat horizons. The weather in Sacramento was as extreme as the landscape. There were two rivers, and these rivers would flood in the winter and run dry in the summer. Winter was cold rain and tulle fog. Summer was 100 degrees, 105 degrees, 110 degrees. Those extremes affect the way you deal with the world. It so happens that if you're a writer the extremes show up. They don't if you sell insurance.

Wired for Books

Don Swaim / 1987

From *Book Beat,* broadcast in three parts starting January 25, 1988. © 1988 by Don Swaim. Reprinted by permission.

Don Swaim: Well, the last time I saw you really chat I think you were working away while I was interviewing your husband. I think you were in a room here in New York. I assume, however, you had finished *Miami* by that time, so you were probably embarking on something new. That was in March.

Joan Didion: I can't remember when I finished it. I think I was probably still working on it, in fact, because I think I didn't finish it until May, actually.

DS: Well, they got it out in pretty fast time, then, didn't they?

JD: Yeah, they had seen it as early as November, but I kept adding stuff and making changes.

DS: You are an extensive revisionist.

JD: Yeah, I revise every single page as I go. I just revise and revise and revise and revise. It used to drive our child mad (*laughter*) that we would try to make her do the same thing.

DS: You certainly write tight. Whereas John Gregory Dunne is rather brawling and sprawling in his approach, you are very fastidious and very compact in your writing. Something tells me—now I don't know that much about writing or anything, I'm just a reader, really—but it seems to me to write tight is probably one of the most difficult things you can do. Tell me about your approach to putting words on paper.

JD: Well, generally it's very hard. The first sentence is the hardest part because once you've got the first sentence laid out, then you are committed to going in a certain direction. And until you get it right you haven't got anything, so I usually spend an awful lot of time messing around with the beginning, and then as I get toward the end of something everything is set and it goes very fast. Because also by the time you get near the end of something you know what it's about. When you begin you're just working out in the blue. You don't have any idea what you're doing. In the case of *Miami*, I had spent time down there, I kept going back, I had a lot of notes, I had done a lot of reading. But I had masses and masses and masses and binders full of absolutely unfocused interviews and material, which I didn't have the slightest idea what I wanted to do with. At one time, I thought maybe the focus is the DEA. You could go in a whole lot of different directions. And it's not really until you get about halfway through that you know what direction you're going in.

DS: Well, you've written a political profile of Miami that stretches out to Latin America as well as up to Washington. All of your work—including your novels and your last novel, *Democracy*—everything has a political orientation in your life, doesn't it?
JD: As I have gotten older I seem to have become more rather than less political and tend to see things in political terms, where I didn't when I first started writing.

DS: It's usually the other way around. As people get older they become used to what's going on and less rebellious and more accepting, don't you think?
JD: Well, I'm a slow study (*laughter*). It took me a while to have that sense of putting things together. I was pretty wrapped up in myself when I was in school and that kind of continued for a while.

DS: Your early novels, what approach did they take?
JD: My first novel was written entirely out of, I think, some kind of homesickness. I was living in New York and I kept thinking about California. I was right out of school, so I just started making up a story that involved a whole lot of weather. I would just remember what the weather was like and then I'd do a scene or two in that weather. And then I'd do a scene about rain—really it was just remembering the weather.

DS: You had to put people under those clouds.
JD: Yeah, I put people, but really you're just telling yourself a story. Writing novels is kind of fun because you are keeping yourself entertained at the same time.

DS: It's kind of like working on a puzzle, isn't it? Creating a puzzle for yourself and solving it.

JD: And solving it, yeah. Throwing out a lot of cards and then trying to find a pattern. I mean you just keep throwing new stuff in.

DS: And if it doesn't work, I imagine you sense it in some form.

JD: What you do then is you throw something else down. You enlarge. Rather than start over you put another layer on it.

DS: Kind of like Monopoly.

JD: Or pick-up sticks.

DS: Well, most recently, you have had a preoccupation with Latin America. Tell me, how did this develop?

JD: Yeah, actually it started—there were two main things. I became interested in Miami specifically a long time ago, in the late sixties when in the aftermath of the Kennedy assassination—do you remember Jim Garrison? He was the district attorney in New Orleans and he was conducting an investigation into the assassination, which eventually came to nothing. But the names that kept coming up and the weird stories that kept coming out of that part of the world. All of the people he was dealing with in New Orleans had connections in Miami, and there was a whole underbelly that I'd never seen before. Everybody belonged to a flying club. It was just real news to me, and I started thinking about that part of the world, from the Gulf Coast down around Miami, the whole Caribbean connection. This was a time when people kept saying that California was the face of America's future.

DS: Boy, were they wrong.

JD: Yeah. Living in California then, it didn't seem to me that that was anywhere near where America's future was. There was something going on in the Caribbean that I didn't understand. So I started being interested in it then. Then in 1973 I went to South America for the first time. I'd been to Mexico and further down but not to South America. And I kind of played around then with the idea of doing something down there, doing a book about Latin America. But instead I wrote a novel. I got typhoid, I came home, I wrote *A Book of Common Prayer,* which was about an imagined Central American country. But it interests me down there. Gradually, over the years I have started answering some of the questions that I kept asking myself in the beginning of that.

DS: I believe you say in *Miami* that Miami is kind of a microcosm of all Latin America. You say that in effect, don't you?

JD: Well, it certainly is our Latin American city. Everything that happens in the United States that concerns Latin America goes through Miami.

DS: Well, I think you say somewhere in here that somebody asks, "How is Miami doing?" And the response is, "Well, how is South America doing?"

JD: Tell me when South America is going to turn around. It's a really international city. It's international in a way that I think no other American city except possibly Honolulu is. In Honolulu you get that sense of Asia. But Honolulu is very isolated, it's in the middle of the Pacific and it will remain isolated. Miami is right here. It's two and three-quarters hours on the airplane from New York. So it is pretty interesting that there is so little apprehension of it outside south Florida.

DS: The mosaic that you create in *Miami*—well, the focus, really—is on the Latin American community there. Their involvement in the politics, their control of the economics, and of course the split between the Latins and the Anglos. But I think the Latins are now obviously the dominant population.

JD: They are numerically the majority. And they are as well—it is the dominant culture. They are the most active, they are taking charge of the economic institutions. I was primarily interested to begin with in their relationship with Washington. Miami seems in a lot of ways to connect to Washington, to connect in ways that other American cities don't. Practically every Cuban you talk to in Miami has at some point worked for the government, for the CIA. There's been a lot of government action down in Miami, which is interesting. In a way the city as it exists is a product of things that are done in Washington, Washington foreign policy.

DS: Something surprised me, something you said just a moment ago. You said when you started going to Miami, collecting all this data, you weren't sure what you were going to write about. I mean, how can you start a book or begin to research a book and not know—

JD: Well, I knew that there was going to be a connection with Washington, but I didn't know how to go about it exactly. As I say, I thought maybe the connection was through the drug stuff. Then, ultimately, that didn't interest me so much. If you knew exactly what a book was going to be before you started you'd be so bored that you wouldn't have the heart to continue it. I mean you really have to kind of keep surprising yourself.

DS: Well, let's go back to Sacramento, California, where you grew up. What was your childhood like?
JD: It was very comfortable, very . . . I don't know. Have you ever been to Sacramento?

DS: No, I haven't.
JD: It's totally flat. That sounds odd.

DS: You mean geographically.
JD: Geographically, it is flat. Every place you look there's a flat horizon. And I think that tends to give people who grow up there a certain view of the world. I like to see a flat horizon still. We lived on the ocean for a while and that was very reassuring to me. I didn't care about the ocean itself or the beach but the horizon—that's what I missed when I moved away. I miss the horizon of Sacramento.

DS: It's as though you have better control.
JD: You're grounded, that's right.

DS: Your view isn't blocked by something else and you can see what's on the other side.
JD: I get very uneasy in hills, you know (*laughter*).

DS: Did you grow up in a literary household?
JD: No.

DS: What did your mother and father do?
JD: My father, during World War II, was in the Air Corps. He was a finance officer. And then afterwards he was in the real estate business. He went back as a reserve officer at one point. And what he does [now] is he buys and sells real estate. He's not a broker. He just buys things and then he sells them.

DS: Did you have some inkling in your childhood that you might be a writer?
JD: Yeah, I wanted to be a writer, but you really don't know how to do it. I kept playing around with it and imagining being a writer, which usually involved having a quote-unquote Manhattan penthouse. That was my image of being a writer.

DS: Don't all writers have Manhattan penthouses and homes in California?
JD: (*Laughter*) So I was always trying to write things, but it's a very long, long—I was talking to some college kids yesterday and we were talking about the impossibility of imagining when you are in school that you will be able to operate out of school, that you will be able to do what you want to do. It's a terrible, terrible crushing burden, particularly as graduation approaches and you know suddenly that all those things you want to do you're going to have to try to do them and be tested against other people. It's really scary. I think being in college is the hardest time for children. I have a child in college now.

DS: Yes, but particularly a writer, a young writer. I'm always amazed, overwhelmed when a young writer comes up with a good book, particularly a good book of fiction, because when I look back at my immature post-adolescence, I really didn't have very much to say. Or if I did I don't think it was very important.
JD: That's the way I feel about myself too. I had nothing to say and I didn't know how to say it, moreover.

DS: By the same token, I know sixty-year-old people who don't have anything to say.
JD: Well, that's true (*laughter*). I'm always amazed when someone very young manages to control—there are so many ways you can go wrong when you write something down. I was amazed, for example, Brett Ellis seems to me amazing in the amount of control he has in that book that he wrote when he was still in school.

DS: *Less than Zero.*
JD: Yeah.

DS: Yeah, well, you know, that book had problems, though. It was a very thin book, which is understandable. But it really was a revision of several other efforts. And I haven't read the second book, but his second book, according to the reviews I read of it, is a carbon copy of his first. But I don't know, he may develop into something.
JD: He's got a lot of talent, I think.

DS: But people like Stryon, when he wrote *Lie Down in Darkness* when he was twenty-six.
JD: Great book.

DS: That book still holds up today, and I just wonder if he, at twenty-six, could he have been faking it?

JD: Isn't that amazing. I certainly didn't have any of that kind of control at twenty-six. My first novel was published when I was twenty-eight or twenty-nine and it doesn't have any control at all.

DS: It doesn't have any control?

JD: No, no. I didn't know how to do anything.

DS: Have you read it lately?

JD: No, I haven't read it lately. But I knew at the time that I didn't know how to do it and I knew I had wanted to do a novel that had a fluid time thing, where everything was happening out of sequence.

DS: This is the one about weather?

JD: This is *Run River*, yeah. It was the one about weather. And I tried doing it that way and it was unreadable. Finally, in desperation I straightened out the chronology. But that wasn't the way I had wanted it to be. Later, I did write novels that were out of sequence and everything happened. But by then I knew how to do it. It's very discouraging to look back at things where you didn't know how to do things.

DS: Oh! Well, I haven't read your first novel, but in reading *Democracy*—

JD: It goes all over the map, yeah.

DS:—it's in and out of sequence. What's fascinating to me is that of course everything's out of sequence in *Democracy*, and yet when you finish reading it you know what happened as if you hadn't read it out of sequence. It's almost like life itself. Life is out of sequence. You determine things that happen around you by bits and pieces and you put them together. Even at the end of the day you find out what somebody has done at one point, somebody else.

JD: And you put it together.

DS: So when you finish *Democracy* there is a story that has a beginning, a middle, and an end. When you first start reading it it's not that way at all. There's the great puzzle that is being solved for us as we read.

JD: It requires a little reader participation to put it together. You have to read more actively probably. But it was too hard for me to do with a first book. I didn't learn how to do it actually until I did it in *A Book of Common Prayer* for the first time.

DS: I was reading a rather ambitious first novel by a young man named Bruce Duffy last week, and it's a well-done novel. But the thing that drove me up the wall about it was that he didn't use quotation marks when he came to structures of dialogue.

JD: It's hard to read, yeah.

DS: As a speed reader—by the end of this week I will have done eight interviews, almost all fiction—and for someone who must read fast, I need those quotation marks. I don't know if a writer has to be too cute. I mean, quotation marks are there for a purpose.

JD: Do you remember a French novel that was all dialogue? It was called *The Dinner Party*. I think it was Claude Mauriac. And it took place entirely at a dinner table and it was all dialogue but none of it was attributed, so you had to figure out who was speaking just from context. There were eight or ten people at the table. That was quite a lot of work to no real point.

DS: Well, who published your first novel?

JD: Ivan Obolensky.

DS: He's not around anymore, is he?

JD: He is. He's a consultant, he's an analyst on publishing stocks for a brokerage house, I think.

DS: I think Jeffrey [Gregory—*ed.*] McDonald, who is going to come in today. I think his first books were published by . . .

JD: By Obolensky, really? Actually, that house only existed for a short time. It was a nice small house.

DS: So, uh, tell me about college. Where'd you go to school?

JD: I went to Berkeley.

DS: And studied . . .

JD: I studied English.

DS: With the intention of being . . .

JD: Well, if you were studying English at Berkeley in the fifties, it was assumed that you were going to go on to graduate school and teach English. That's what people who did English did. So I spent all my time under these false colors. I mean I wasn't interested in really going to graduate school and I didn't want to teach. But that was simply where everything channeled. I mean, I loved Berkeley. I loved being there. I loved the campus. I loved everything about it. But I realized after I got out that I probably should have majored in history. I would have been better off. I went back to Berkeley in 1975 and taught in the English department on a special thing. I had a fellowship. And it was this extraordinary experience of going back to some place that's a very emotional period of your life, and walking back into that life nineteen years later, or whatever it was, in this totally reversed position. I was in the English department, but I wasn't a student anymore. And I was living in The Faculty Club for this month I was there. And the Faculty Club at Berkeley is right in the middle of campus and at night I would be the only person on campus, I was the only person staying there after the library closed. There I would be. And it was extraordinary. I slipped right back into student depressions, you know. I started wearing a dirty raincoat again, kind of walked around eating—I had nuts in my pocket. It was really odd, and very gratifying in a way to close a circle.

DS: Well, you resist[ed] the impulse to retrench completely. You moved on. What happened after college?
JD: Well, this sounds so silly, but I won a contest. *Vogue* used to have a contest for college seniors and the prize was a job, and so I was offered a job at *Vogue,* so I came to New York and worked for over eight years. It was my only real job.

DS: What kind of job was that?
JD: Well, when I first came I didn't have any particular skills. I was so naïve. I can remember on the personnel sheet where you were asked what languages you can read putting down Middle English. I really was still very much the product of an academic environment. So I was just mainly in a room and they gave me a lot of bound volumes of *Vogue* and I read them for about a year. It seems to me that's all I did. And once in a while I would get a little assignment of some kind and do it.

DS: Well, it was a job.
JD: It was great. It was $45 a week.

DS: And in New York. You could have been working for a weekly shopper in Toledo.

JD: It was terrific, and they were really nice. They were like a family and they kind of took care of me and made sure I called my mother and stuff like that. After a while I moved into the feature department and was writing copy in the feature department and became an associate editor in the feature department. I loved it. I learned a lot of stuff. Allene Talmey, who has died since, was the feature editor then, and she really helped me a lot. She would mark up copy and make me do it over and over and over and she would just be furious if there were an extra word or if there were a verb that didn't work or if something didn't work. I mean, everything we were talking about was an eight-line caption, maybe, but it had to work. I really learned a lot from her. I learned a lot at *Vogue,* particularly from her.

DS: I think you're still applying some of those techniques, aren't you?
JD: Yeah, I still go through copy and mark it up with big Xs the way she used to mark up mine.

DS: How did you meet John Gregory Dunne?
JD: I was working at *Vogue* and he was working at *Time* and we had mutual friends. We'd had mutual friends and had known each other a long time before we ever began going out.

DS: Had you at this point published?
JD: I had not published at the time I knew him. I'd known him since I was about twenty-three, I guess. It wasn't until after I published *Run River* that we began going out.

DS: Well, I guess I have to ask you this question: What is it like living with another writer in the house? Do you struggle over who's going to get the typewriter on a given day?
JD: Uh, no.

DS: Of course you'd have two typewriters now.
JD: (*Laughter*) Just about. Actually we've got two computers now. I don't know what it would be like not being married to a writer. We've been married twenty-three years and it's like having an editor in the house. And if I weren't married to a writer, if I were married to someone who came home at the end of the day and came in from a different world he would be not too happy to find me wrapped up in this world I was doing. It's very convenient

from both of our points of view to have us both doing the same thing more or less, in the same business.

DS: You don't critique each other's work, do you?

JD: Oh yeah, oh yeah. He's my editor, really, and my first reader. And I am his.

DS: How can that be? He writes so differently than you do. And when you read his stuff, do you edit his stuff too? And you don't strike out sentences and adjectives and all that?

JD: No, no, no. We each know how the other works. But sometimes you have an idea of how it could work better. You just have to know whether or not something is working. You can say, "This isn't working."

DS: And he doesn't run screaming out of the room?

JD: Well, sometimes I run screaming out of the room (*laughter*) when he does it to me because he is much more forthright than I am. I tend to just sort of say, "It's terrific, but maybe something's not . . ." He says I don't meet his eyes and then he knows. But he will be very direct and say, "No, this doesn't work. This is out." And it usually makes me quite cross at the moment because you usually know when something's not working, but at the same time you wish somebody would say, "Oh, don't change a word." You wish you would be over with this thing, through with it.

DS: That's wishful thinking, but it seems to me that you two are exceptional, because when it comes to friends and spouses critiquing another's work—for example, I have a friend, a colleague who is now a full-time writer but was working here at CBS, and he gave me a manuscript that he was working on at the time and I made all sorts of notes, I made about six pages of notes. I mean, there were lots of flaws in this book, which was never published. And I made the mistake of sitting down with him and telling him and he didn't speak to me for three weeks. He didn't want me to criticize it.

JD: Nobody wants it.

DS: He wanted praise.

JD: That's a lot easier from someone you're living with because you know that, really, you have a sense of trust that you just don't have with other people, even the best friends. It's possible not to speak to a best friend for three weeks. It's not possible not to speak to somebody in your house for three weeks.

DS: You want to bet? (*laughter*) I know people who haven't spoken for three years!

JD: I don't have the stamina for that.

DS: Now, you and your husband have never collaborated on a book, but you've done a lot of movies together. How does that work?

JD: Well, it works fine. I can't imagine not collaborating on a movie because it's not like writing. It's like doing something else. It's like working on a puzzle or something. The actual words don't matter very much. What matters is the structure, the stuff you can talk out. And also because it is going to be somebody else's movie there's not a lot of ego involved. Your name is not going to be the thing that people—you are not alone responsible for this, so it's possible for people to share the work.

DS: You know they're going to change everything around anyway.

JD: Change everything or maybe not change a word, but there will be other people's work involved. I remember a movie we wrote once in which not a word was changed. The script was exactly as we wrote it, that was the way it was shot. Yet it was a totally different movie than what we had in mind just because of variations in the acting.

DS: It was supposed to take place in midtown Manhattan, but it turned out in rural Indiana.

JD: (*Laughter*) Location, that's right.

DS: Well, I just can't imagine your collaborating on a book with your husband.

JD: No, I can't either. Nor could he. It would be out of the question.

DS: One of you could do the research, I guess, the other the writing. But I don't even see that. Well, now, you have gone from—mostly you've been concentrating on the nonfiction recently more than your novels. Is this going to be a pattern?

JD: No, I have done only one nonfiction book since *Democracy*, and now I'm going back to a novel.

DS: Two.

JD: No, *Salvador* preceded *Democracy*. I'm very clear on that because I decided to go to El Salvador at a moment when I thought I could not possibly finish *Democracy*, so I was trying to get away from it. But I'm going back to a novel now.

DS: Do you always have a project in the works?
JD: Yeah, uh-huh. Sometimes more actively so than others.

DS: You live part of the time in California, part of the time in New York. Where do you do the most work?
JD: I have been doing more work in California because the house is larger and it's easier for me to work if there's more room.

DS: Why? Your books are so small, why do you need a big house?
JD: (*Laughter*)

DS: It should be the other way around.
JD: It is just easier for me to operate. The apartment in New York is small for two people to be working in.

DS: You ought to see mine. I'd think your apartment was huge.
JD: But you're working right here, you see. You're not working in your apartment.

DS: I work in my apartment. My apartment is an extension of my office here, and I have more room there than I do here, actually. I'm completely out of space. What kind of computer do you use?
JD: Oh, I just learned. I have a little laptop, a Zenith. And I'm so crazy about it. I cried for three weeks trying to learn it. I thought I'd do it, and then I started doing it and it was so hard and so irritating and so frustrating, but at the same time I knew that it was much easier to use if I knew how to use it than a typewriter. So I couldn't really go back to the typewriter, but on the other hand I couldn't learn this, so it was a whole crisis.

DS: Oh, yeah. People don't realize it. They say, "I'm going to make my life better as a writer." Then they get the computer and they find out that you have to learn the computer in the same way you learn how to type. As a matter of fact, you have to learn how to type before you can learn the computer. And people who don't know how to type have to learn that and then they have to learn the computer on top of it. So it's like half a year of education.
JD: You know how literal it is. It's much more literal than anything I've ever had any dealings with, than anything or anybody. It's quite a new way for me

to think, to adjust to something so literal, that will do exactly what you tell it if you tell it in unmistakably clear terms. Most of our dealings, we tend to shortcut them. We tend to talk in shorthand and to give directions in shorthand. It's like people dictating letters and saying, "Sincerely, et cetera." A lot of our dealings with other people and with most machines are "Sincerely, et cetera," but with a computer you have to do it all the way. It's a whole other way of thinking. It's quite interesting.

DS: Does it have a spell checker?
JD: It has all that stuff.

DS: That's sensational, isn't it?
JD: Yeah.

DS: In a novel you can change the name of a character John to Bob by pressing a button all the way through.
JD: Yeah, the spell check is a little irritating because it is so literal that it stops and gives a query on every word it doesn't know, and it doesn't know a lot of words.

DS: Well, if you're using a Zenith laptop it probably doesn't have too much memory, so it probably has a dictionary that has maybe 40,000 words, which is not very big.
JD: Whatever the WordPerfect dictionary is.

DS: I have a computer that uses Microsoft Word and it has a dictionary that has 90,000 words, which is one of the larger dictionaries. That's really helpful. And another thing that this one does, and it didn't do before, it will list plurals.
JD: Oh, really?

DS: You might write "fathers," and it wouldn't let you go by "fathers" because it's not in the dictionary, but the new one has a bigger dictionary that allows that.
JD: Yeah.

DS: Well, I think my listeners, when they read *Miami,* will have a whole new insight on that city. I know I didn't know very much about that city myself. I'm planning to go down in February. I haven't been back to Miami for many years. More than twenty years ago, when I was there, I know it had a large

Latin population, but nothing the way it is today. And I know it wasn't as volatile as it is today. So a lot of the sociological, political changes I'm going to be monitoring by reading the papers down there, guided to a certain degree by your book. So I want to thank you very, very much for coming in.

JD: Thank you.

The Salon Interview: Joan Didion

Dave Eggers / 1996

From *Salon,* October 28, 1996. © 1966 by Salon Media Group, Inc. Reprinted by permission.

Joan Didion's new novel, *The Last Thing He Wanted*, is her first in twelve years. Set in 1984, it centers on Elena McMahon, an American journalist who gets tangled up in the covert sales of American arms in Central America. It is sparsely written and tightly plotted and fiercely intelligent—all the sorts of things we've come to expect from Didion.

Some things that you probably know but if not will be helpful in enjoying this interview:

- Didion is married to John Gregory Dunne, and has been for a long time. When she says "we," he makes "we."
- Though she no longer writes the sort of personal-social essays that made up books like *The White Album* and *Slouching Towards Bethlehem*, she still contributes journalism and critical essays to magazines like *The New Yorker* and *The New York Review of Books*.
- In person she is very small. She is also graceful, personable, warm, and funny.

Dave Eggers: With *The Last Thing He Wanted*, I read that you weren't sure how it was going to turn out until you were finished with it.

Joan Didion: No, no I wasn't. I wanted to do a very, very tight plot, just a single thread—you wouldn't even see the thread and then when you pulled it at the end everything would fall into place. That was the intention there. But you would go mad if you tried to plot that closely ahead of time. So essentially what you have to do, I found, is you have to make it up every day as you go along. And then you have to play the cards you already have on the table—you have to deal with what you've already said. Quite often, you've got yourself into things that seem to lead nowhere, but if you force yourself to deal with them, that was the discipline of it.

For example, one of the first things I had started with in this book was the idea of this woman walking off a campaign. Because I'd covered some campaigns in '88 and '92, I wanted to use some of that sense of a campaign. So then, I didn't know, then she would go to Miami to see her father. Then, I couldn't figure out where she'd been. Then, I decided she ought to be from Los Angeles and had been married to someone in the oil business. That kind of gave me a fresh start. But then I was having to get her from Los Angeles to being a political reporter, right? It was a really hard thing to do. It was also a lot of fun.

Eggers: There were certain chapters where it does sound like you're starting from scratch almost, when you start hearing about Elena's dreams, for example.

Didion: Yeah, I mean, I was just sitting there wondering what I could do that day. Sometimes, also, you just feel it's right to step back from it a little bit. Otherwise it's going to get linear, "and then she said, and then she did . . ." It doesn't keep you awake to write it.

Eggers: While your fiction seems to be getting increasingly lean, your essays seem to be moving in the opposite direction.

Didion: They're getting denser and denser. There's a whole lot of stuff going on in a piece—you're trying to think it through. Generally, you think about a question or a situation in a more complex way than you would make a scene. Novels are almost like music or poetry—they just come to me in simple sentences, whereas I think my pieces get more and more complex ever since I've started using a computer.

Eggers: What do you use?

Didion: I use an IBM Thinkpad. I just use it like a typewriter, but when I started using it in 1987, I thought I won't be able to write anymore, so I thought I'd go back to the typewriter. But you couldn't go back to the typewriter after using the computer, so finally after about a month I got proficient enough that I could actually work on it without being distracted by it, and in fact then it started making me a whole lot more logical than I ever had been. Because the computer was so logical, it was always right, I was wrong . . . and the time saved.

Before I started working on a computer, writing a piece would be like making something up every day, taking the material and never quite knowing where you were going to go next with the material. With a computer it was less like painting and more like sculpture, where you start with a block of something and then start shaping it.

Eggers: You feel like it's just there . . .

Didion: It's just there, and sometimes you'll find yourself—you get one paragraph partly right, and then you'll go back and work on the other part. It's a different thing.

Eggers: Your work feels like it was written by a slow writer. I mean that in the best possible way.

Didion: Over the course of several years I had false starts on this novel several times. I couldn't get anywhere with it. Then I had this block of time last fall from the end of August until Christmas, so I just decided I would try to finish it in that period. So I went back and I started, and I did finish it about Christmas time, but that was about as fast as I could work. And a lot of it turned out to already be done in note form to hang together. So this was just running it through with the thread.

Eggers: There is a character in the book named Bob Weir. Are you a Grateful Dead fan?

Didion: [*laughs*] No, that is where that name comes from, isn't it? I had totally forgotten that. No, I had no idea, I knew there was something just right about that name.

Eggers: Elena resembles, in certain ways, some of your other characters from some of your other novels, in that she finds herself in the middle of this huge life change, and it's seemingly irreversible, and yet she goes with it. What does that pattern mean to you?

Didion: I don't know, it's nothing I want to examine too closely. Every time I do it, I think it's brand new. It comes to me in a flash! [*laughs*] It would certainly make things easier if I remembered, but it's—I guess all novels are dreams of what might happen or dreams of what you don't want to happen. When you're working on them, it's very much like a dream you're moving in. So, to some extent, obviously, the same characters are going to keep populating your dreams.

Eggers: Have you ever done something like Elena does here—walked off a campaign, reinvented yourself?

Didion: Not really, no. But you can see the possibility, it's something you might be afraid of happening. It's definitely something you don't want to happen. I don't want to happen. That's what I would take from it.

Eggers: I read somewhere that you identified yourself as a libertarian.
Didion: I was explaining to somebody what kind of Republican I had been. That was essentially why I had been feeling estranged from the Republican Party per se, because my whole point of view had been libertarian. I mean, I wouldn't call it totally "on the program" libertarian.

Eggers: You don't vote the ticket?
Didion: [*laugh*] No . . . I think the attraction was that it was totally free. It was totally based on individual rights, which, as a Westerner, I was responsive to. Then I started realizing there was a lot of ambiguity in the West's belief that it had a stronghold on rugged individualism, since basically it was created by the federal government. So I haven't come to any hard conclusion, here.

Eggers: Are you watching the campaign? What do you think of Clinton?
Didion: Well, he's the luckiest man alive, isn't he? He seems to be lucky, which I guess in a lot of cultures has been what people wanted. Luck had a kind of totemic power, that made you the leader.

Eggers: I read your review of Bob Woodward's *The Choice*, in *The New York Review of Books*. It seemed that his lengthy descriptions of his reporterly methods got under your skin.
Didion: Yes. There's a certain kind of reporting of a book that when you're casually reading through you think you've missed something, you're not informed here, you've totally missed the point, there must be something more to this than meets the eye. So then I started reading *The Choice* and I had been actually following the campaign in a way until then, so I did know something about it, and I thought, what's going on here? There's nothing here we don't know. And even then, I would sort of doze off every now and then and think "I must be missing this—there must be more to this than I'm finding."

Eggers: You and your husband wrote the screenplay for *Up Close and Personal.* How do you think it turned out?

Didion: Well, it turned out—from the beginning, what it was supposed to be was a vehicle for two movie stars, and that's what it was.

Eggers: You have no illusions, it seems, about the Hollywood game.
Didion: Well, if you don't know how to play it you shouldn't be in it. It's always sort of amused me.

Eggers: I just read an interview with Charles Schultz, the creator of Peanuts. He's a billionaire, of course, and he was asked what his idea of success was—if he considered himself "successful." He said something like, "Yes, because now I feel like I can go into any bookstore, and if I see a book I really like, I can buy it." I thought that was really beautiful. Do you consider yourself successful?
Didion: I never feel particularly successful. I always feel like I've not quite done it right, that I ought to be doing better or something. In terms of work, I never felt that I've done it right. I always want to have done it differently, to have done it better, a different way, unlike Charles Schulz. So I don't know. The one time I felt successful was when he [Schultz] put my daughter Quintana's name in a cartoon.

Joan Didion, One Week after 9/11

Jon Wiener / 2001

From the *Los Angeles Review of Books* (www.lareviewofbooks.org), September 11, 2003.

Joan Didion was on one of the first flights from New York to California after 9/11. She had been scheduled to speak in Los Angeles and San Francisco about a new book, *Political Fictions*, which contained eight pieces on the American political landscape from 1988 to 2000, all of them published previously in *The New York Review of Books*. She was sixty-seven, and had already published four [five—ed.] novels (including *Play It As It Lays* in 1970) and five nonfiction books (including *Salvador* in 1983 and *Miami* in 1987). *Political Fictions* had taken on a sudden new significance when I spoke with her about it one week after 9/11. In our conversation, she seemed unusually halting and hesitant.

Jon Wiener: You flew from New York City to California today—what was that like?
Joan Didion: It was uneventful. The plane was about half full, and nothing happened.

JW: You live in New York City—what was your day like on Tuesday 9/11?
JD: As it was happening, we were in shock—all day. But the shock on Tuesday was not as dramatic as the shock when we woke up on Wednesday morning and realized that it was real. We went downtown on Tuesday night to a birthday party. It was very hard to get downtown, obviously. The party wasn't festive, it was quite somber, but it felt very good to be with people. I think everybody was there for that reason.

JW: Have you been downtown in the week since then?

JD: Below Houston you have a very strong sense of—of the nearness of it. We live uptown, but Wednesday night the wind changed, and there was a smell unlike anything I have ever smelled. All night long. And then the next day it rained.

JW: The news today is that President George W. Bush has just launched—
JD: "Operation Infinite Justice." Yes.

JW: You've always paid close attention to our political rhetoric. What do you make of "Operation Infinite Justice"?
JD: At first it sounded like we were immediately going to be bombing someone. Then it sounded like it was going to be something like another war on drugs, a very amorphous thing with a heightened state of rhetoric and some threat to civil liberties.

JW: You started this series of essays with the 1988 election, [Dukakis] versus Bush, Senior—and you write that the story has been pretty much the same ever since: the American political process does not offer citizens a voice, or much of a choice; instead it is designed by and for "that handful of insiders who invent, year in and year out, the narrative of public life." Of course that narrative was disrupted last week.
JD: It was disrupted, but if you listen to TV, everyone is trying to shoehorn it into their existing agenda. I picked up *The National Review* yesterday, where [Ann] Coulter was saying, "We should invade their countries, kill their leaders, and convert them to Christianity." Even if we thought that was the way to go, how would we go about it? Put them in a twelve-step program? Put them in Teen Challenge? We're seeing a lot of the patriotism of Americans, but we're in danger of seeing it drowned in a surge of jingoism. Which is kind of—frightening.

JW: You wrote in your book that, in the political developments since 1988, you saw a "nostalgia for an imagined America." Is that continuing this week?
JD: I think so. People are talking about "America losing its innocence." How many times can America lose its innocence? In my lifetime we've heard that we've lost our innocence half a dozen times at least.

JW: President Bush in his press conference yesterday cited the poster in the Old West that said "Wanted dead or alive." What do you make of that as political rhetoric?

JD: Both *The New York Times* and *The Washington Post* today carried stories out of the White House about how the president's "dead or alive" language quote "is his own." It is, and it isn't his own. Every morning there is a meeting with Bush, Cheney, Condoleez[z]a Rice, Karen Hughes, and others, in which they determine what the words and emotional cues should be for that day's communications. When Karen Hughes briefed reporters on this, she gave them an example of how the president really shaped these words himself. But it was essentially a matter of changing "Get them on the run" to "Smoke them out and get them running." It was not a change in spirit.

JW: *The New York Times* quoted a Republican advisor who said this is "his natural rhetoric, which is very much regular-guy language and is very appealing."
JD: [*Laughs*] Yes.

JW: I gather you don't find it very appealing.
JD: I keep thinking his family is from Connecticut.

JW: You've got the wrong idea there: he's from Midland, which is in Texas!
  Today we read that "In an effort to avoid a partisan debate after the terrorist attacks last week, Senate Democrats have agreed to withdraw a budget provision that would have restricted [. . .] spending on missile defense."
JD: There's no difference between the parties, is there? We don't have an actual argument. We have two parties that calibrate everything they do to attract a very small group called "the target voters." As for the rest of us, I don't think it's too strong to say we have been dis[en]franchised.

JW: Most pundits emphasized the unique and unprecedented qualities of the Bush v. Gore contest in Florida that ended the 2000 election—but you wrote that the events in Florida were "not only entirely predictable, but entirely familiar." What do you mean?
JD: It was entirely predictable: at the most immediate level, the election was that close because both candidates had run the same campaign directed at the same small number of people. Florida had a certain poetry to it; it was like a haiku of what the process had become.

Berkeley Alumna Discusses Politics after *Fictions*

Rebecca Meyer / 2001

From *The Daily Californian,* October 19, 2001. © 2001 by *The Daily Californian*. Reprinted by permission.

Daily Californian: What do you remember about being a student at Cal?
Joan Didion: I loved Berkeley. It was like waking up. The whole way I deal with politics came out of the English department. They taught a form of literary criticism which was based on analyzing texts in a very close way. If you start analyzing the text of a newspaper or a political commentator on CNN using this same approach of close textual analysis, you come to understand it in a different way. It's not any different from reading Henry James.

DC: In "The West Wing of Oz," you talk about elected officials using international affairs as a set for the theater of domestic politics. Do you see that going on right now?
JD: In one way it's a hugely different thing because we didn't initiate this—we were attacked. But I do notice that a lot of the response to it has had elements of—when Bush gave his first address to the nation, it was reviewed before and after as to how it would play in terms of his domestic ratings. The speech, which was a response to the actual attack, was being construed as part of an ongoing political campaign.

DC: You portray American democracy as fairly bankrupt. If you see through all this theater in the name of politics, what keeps you tuned in? Where do you find the strength to indict the fable-makers rather than just tuning out?
JD: I keep thinking that when everybody notices the inconsistencies, the way things don't add up, there will be a change. It's a romantic idea, I suppose, but I keep thinking it. Just in the weeks since the book was published,

in fact, I've gotten a heartening response. A lot of people are starting to think along the same lines.

DC: It sounds like it was hard for you to start writing about politics.
JD: It was. It was a whole learning experience. I didn't have any confidence that I could do it, and I didn't have the access. I had always stayed away from stories which a lot of people were covering because temperamentally I didn't like to fight for the interview. I was kind of forced to do it from outside.

DC: Did it get easier?
JD: Yes, because I had some history with it. In 1988 everything was really shocking, really stunning. Because I was so shocked, a lot of things became clear to me. When I came back to it when I was covering the 1992 campaign, I thought, "I don't want to do this again—it's all the same stuff. I already said this." But then I realized that there was a virtue in pointing out that it was the same stuff and looking at it again.

DC: One of the great things about *Political Fictions* is the way you allow things we all see but take for granted to be disconcerting to you. What scares you about what's happening now?
JD: Not too many things actually scare me, but I'm as anxious as the next person, maybe more so than most people. There comes a moment when you recognize that you can't control things. I was a child when the atomic bomb was dropped, then we had the Cold War, etc., which seemed very hot and urgent at the time. And I was afraid until I was in my twenties that I wouldn't wake up in the morning because the world would have ended.

We had all these silly drills of getting under our desks when I was a child. You got under your desk, put one arm over your eyes and one arm over your brain stem. Even a child could see that this wasn't going to save us. (*laughs*)

There was a letter in *The New York Times* a few days ago from a reader who believed that most of the public's frustration was that they couldn't do anything. So this reader suggested that they tell people what to do, like set up programs where people can volunteer in flag factories. That sounds just like putting one arm over your eyes and one arm over your brain stem.

Revelle Forum at the Neurosciences Institute: Joan Didion

Michael A. Bernstein / 2002

From the Revelle Forum at the Neuroscience Institute, December 2, 2002. © 2002 by UCSD-TV. Reprinted by permission.

Our distinguished guest this evening, Joan Didion, is a very rare individual. I noticed she's a fifth-generation Californian who actually moved east to New York City. This makes her quite unique, of course. A native of Sacramento, she received a bachelor's degree from a relatively obscure campus of the University of California, which I'm told is located somewhere on the eastern shores of the San Francisco Bay. Her remarkable career as an essayist, novelist, screenwriter has spanned well over three decades. Ms. Didion's fiction includes *Run River, Play It As It Lays, A Book of Common Prayer, Democracy*, and *The Last Thing He Wanted*. Her nonfiction includes *Slouching Towards Bethlehem, The White Album, Salvador, Miami*, and *[After] Henry*. Ms. Didion's screenplays, which she coauthored with her husband, the well-known writer John Gregory Dunne are also very well known. There was *The Panic in Needle Park*, which was released in 1971. And then following, *Play It As It Lays, A Star Is Born, True Confessions, Hills like White Elephants*,[1] and *Up Close and Personal*. Ms. Didion has lectured at many colleges and universities across the country, including Stanford, Bard, UCLA, Yale, and the graduate school of journalism at Columbia University. And, oh yes, Berkeley, of course. In addition to the execution of her many independent writing projects, she is often a regular contributor to the *New Yorker* magazine and to the *New York Review of Books*. Ms. Didion's work has garnered many accolades and awards, among them the Edward MacDowell Medal in 1996 and the Columbia Journalism Award just a couple of years ago. Most recently, her new book, *Political Fictions*, received the prestigious George Polk Journalism Award. It is indeed this latest work, *Political Fictions*, that captures our attention this evening. This collection of essays, first published by Knopf last year, offers a series of penetrating, subversive, often hilarious, and always arresting assessments of recent American political history and of contemporary American political culture. Ms. Didion, it is a great pleasure to have you with us tonight. Thank you. Ladies and gentlemen, please join me in welcoming someone who a recent critic has described as "the freshest application of an acute literary intelligence to the political scene since Norman Mailer gave up going to demonstrations over three decades ago."

Michael A. Bernstein: The focus of these essays, in *Political Fictions,* is primarily the last three presidential elections. There are a few other items addressed. And the major theme in your book concerns what you describe as the growing disconnect between the electorate and what you see as a growing, permanent political class.

Joan Didion: Right. I mean, it wasn't called the disconnect by me or anybody else until the year of the impeachment, right, but that's what in 1988 we were seeing. We were seeing this political class, this political mechanism, the political process that was so isolated that it seemed to be designed entirely to perpetuate itself. And it was impenetrable.

Bernstein: But it's also your central argument that this political class, these insiders, these professionals who serve our candidates for office, or political leaders.

Didion: I write about them, yeah.

Bernstein: They become increasingly obsessed with a shrinking portion of the electorate, correct?

Didion: A shrinking portion of the electorate actually votes, and they are entirely focused on the most likely to vote. And since the people most likely to vote in, say, a primary election are people who have an agenda and can be organized to get to the polls on the basis of that agenda, it has made a very skewed kind of politics. So we have candidates who represent a very narrow agenda usually. And the rest of the electorate loses interest in the general.

Bernstein: That gets us to the foundation of your particular arresting statement in the book that the notion of choice is one of the great fictions of our political system.

Didion: Is the central fiction, yeah. With two parties determined to attract exactly the same voter, and to obscure any discernable difference between themselves, there is no choice.

Bernstein: So we then have the Tweedle-dumlicans and the Tweedle-deemocrats, who in some sense then—

Didion: Now, do you notice the whole question in the past weeks of what potential candidates in 2004 said about Iraq was talked about in the papers and on CNN and wherever you encountered it, was talked about as "positioning themselves." Kerry was said to be positioning himself. The idea that he might have an honest thought about it . . . (*laughter*)

Bernstein: Isn't it also true that this rush for the middle, this rush to a kind of blandness that won't offend for the sake of electoral success, is also characterized by candidates and their staff becoming obsessed with the outliers of their constituencies. You make the point in one of your essays that during the Clinton campaigns, one of the great obsessions of the Clinton staff was to find out what was on the minds of Democrats who had voted for Reagan.

Didion: Oh, the Reagan Democrats are on everybody's mind still. Now they're called the swing vote. Those people are absolutely central to the process, and yet they aren't. They're a very small group of people, really.

Bernstein: And then the candidates, if I'm reading you correctly, are not really speaking to their core constituents. And in fact may ignore them for long periods of the campaign.

Didion: No, no, no, no, no. There was something astonishing that I came across when I was doing one of these pieces, which was the head of the Democratic Leadership Council actually said with pleasure that in the 2000 election finally the parties had achieved parity. Well, what does that mean? It means there's no difference between them.

Bernstein: They're not distinguishable. Let's talk a bit about this issue of voter apathy. You've already mentioned it. The voter participation rate in the United States in national elections is always astonishingly low, certainly by any global comparison. And I wondered to what extent you see this apathy or disengagement as a direct product of this insider class you chronicle?

Didion: I see it as being the product rather than the cause. I think most people see it as being the cause. If we went out and voted . . . I do go out and vote and it doesn't do any good. I don't often find anybody to vote for, I just do it. Like a tick.

Bernstein: Let's talk about voting for a second. There's been a lot of debate in recent years about the mechanisms we have in this country to enable people to vote, or to disable people from voting, in light of the controversies of the last presidential election. I wondered, given the work you've done on these essays, what your opinion was of proposals for example to allow for registration on election day itself.

Didion: Well, I think that would be a very good idea. Making it easier to register, simplifying registration—I mean, to register in New York takes quite a bit of effort on your part. All the motor-voter proposals, I think it's inaction in some states, isn't it?

Bernstein: And then there's the issue of election day itself. We're the only industrialized nation for which election day is not a national holiday.

Didion: We had a mayoral election in New York on September 11, 2001, and a lot of people I knew—my assistant's father was not in the World Financial Center because he'd gone out to vote. It was one of those blessings that comes to voters.

Bernstein: One of the few. Well, I'm curious. You know, there have been proposals that election day be moved to a Sunday, that the polls be open for twenty-four hours.

Didion: Twenty-four hours would be sensible. Also, I know the amount of absentees is becoming a problem. I read a bitter complaint about it the other day, and the fact that large numbers of people were already going to have voted three or four weeks before the election, and so you couldn't throw your television money into the last three or four weeks. I'm not sure that's a bad thing. It's fairly easy to vote absentee if you're voting in California. It's quite hard to vote absentee if you're voting in New York.

Bernstein: There have been some suggestions by political scientists who observe this process that another difficulty we encounter is the activity of the media on elections with exit polling, with efforts to reveal or project results long before the polls have closed.

Didion: You always feel if you live in California, as I've done for most of my life, as if it's over even if they don't say. They're all kind of winking at each other. You know what they think. You know they've got the figures and you can kind of tell what they are before the magic moment.

Bernstein: The invidious memories of Dukakis conceding before the polls had actually closed in California, and how much that angered Democratic voters. Would you think it then a sensible proposal that the media be barred from any commentary until the polls have closed?

Didion: I think it's just one of those things we're going to have to learn to live with. I'm not into barring the media from anything. But I'm not sure they should be allowed to do exit polling. I'm not sure it's useful for anybody. I don't know if the candidates even need to know. I would like people to stay away from the polling place.

Bernstein: Well, let's talk about political campaigning in a little more detail. You poke a lot of fun at the empty and vacuous statements that emanate from all of our candidates for office, and our incumbents, as they aggressively seek out this middle ground and try to appeal to these very small portions of the electorate that they identify as focus groups. I was curious, since you've had the opportunity to spend some time with these campaigners on the trail, if it's your perception that in many respects these individuals never really have a chance to think through the issues.

Didion: I don't think they think through the issues. Their instinctive or reflexive response to an issue is *How can I cover myself on this? How can I not get hurt on this?* I don't think they have time to think through, especially in the heat of the campaign, if something comes up that hasn't come up before.

Bernstein: I recall an essay many years back. John Hersey spent a day with President Ford in the White House. He was given the opportunity simply to trail the president all day. It was evidently a relatively normal day. But nonetheless an opportunity for a working journalist to see the president at work. And Hersey then produced this very long essay for the *New York Times Magazine* one week. It was the whole issue. And in the middle of this description of the president's day, Hersey pulls up short and says, "When does the president think?" It was one meeting after another. It was rushing hither and yon, hearing reports from his staff, but there was never a time where the president was able to sit alone, read, think, jot some notes, formulate his own ideas.

Didion: You see those schedules, and they're all about photo opportunities or other kinds of ops. Nobody remembers this. I remember it because I was teaching at Berkeley in the spring of '75, and I was all by myself in the faculty club most of the time, and I was reading all the papers, and I was mesmerized by the fall of Saigon and the way the story kept changing from edition to edition. I'd run out and get the papers every few hours, it seemed to me. Every story about President Ford's reaction to the fall of Saigon was datelined Palm Desert.

Bernstein: That's more than frightening. On the matter of positioning and molding stories, you have a very powerful chapter in this book, "The West Wing of Oz," where you talk about the Mozote Massacre and the reaction of the Reagan administration to the first news that this massacre may indeed have taken place and in fact might have taken place with knowledge of the American Foreign Relations staff. And you make the point that as the Reagan administration was finally forced to deal with this breaking news, despite its efforts to hold it at arm's length for so long, that President Reagan and his staff were concerned that the nation not suffer from a Vietnam Syndrome, [that it] be strong on the matter of insurgents or terrorists, as we would call them today. Do you think the nation has learned anything of substantial value from the Vietnam experience?

Didion: No, I think we're still there. The whole idea of getting over the Vietnam Syndrome by going to war in Grenada always had a flaw in it. We tried to do it in Central America. There was a point at which people were talking about the war in El Salvador as a perfect model for what we failed to do in Vietnam. What we failed to do there we could do here. But that fell apart in the end of the second administration and the Iran Contra.

Bernstein: There always seems to be the focus on means but not goals.

Didion: Right. They couldn't get the money to do that.

Bernstein: And that was part of the Iran-Contra scandal in the first place. Let's talk a little bit about Ronald Reagan. You spend a fair amount of time in this book talking about Reagan, and in particular you focus on the work of Dinesh D'Souza, who wrote a kind of primer on Ronald Reagan for Americans to learn about what D'Souza described as this remarkable leader. And yet you go to great lengths to show that there's virtually no substance to this argument at all.

Didion: Well, there's no substance to D'Souza's argument. I can imagine, though I've never read it, an argument that Ronald Reagan, despite whatever his flaws were, was a good president, a leader of some sort. I can imagine this argument, not that I've read it. But Dinesh D'Souza didn't make that argument. It was just really dumb.

Bernstein: I share your conviction in that regard. How does one account, then, for pundits like D'Souza—and there are several of them, he's a very prominent example—who issue these books that as we examine them closely come apart in our hands, there's no real foundation to them, but they enjoy all of this attention from the press and from the media when they issue these works.

Didion: Well, there's a whole bunch. D'Souza worked in the White House when he was in his early twenties, and during the first term of the Reagan administration Washington was flooded with children just out of school who were determined to make their own way, and so they did it politically. They weren't going to do what other people their age had done. They were going to take a different line altogether. There was a lot of very, very ideological fervor in Washington at that time, and all those people then turned up in think tanks. Dinesh D'Souza writes a book, it's going to be bought by all those people in think tanks. At the American Enterprise Institute, the Heritage Foundation—there's a certain built-in sale on those books.

Bernstein: There's a built-in audience. It is interesting, though, you demonstrate in your chapter on D'Souza's [book] on Reagan that nevertheless the book was not subjected to any genuine critical scrutiny by the working press, by reviewers. Does that strike you as something new in American public life or do you think this is just the same way of doing things?

Didion: I think it is new. I think that in some ways the critical reading faculty has been atrophied. I don't know how or why.

Bernstein: There's obviously the business pressure in publishing—and in fact in the journalistic world—that make objective news gathering, if there ever was such a thing, and critical analysis of information more and more difficult.

Didion: Journalistically, if you need sources, as reporters tend to need sources, in Washington, you are not going to have those sources unless you write the kinds of stories that they want to see written. You are not going to see your phone calls taken. Ari Fleischer was quoted recently, just something I read over the weekend, having said to somebody in a press conference, just his daily noon briefing. A reporter asked a question, and he didn't like the question, and what he said was something like "Your attitude toward that has been noted in the building."

Bernstein: But that does raise an interesting point. Many of us remember the fairly pugnacious relationship between the White House and the press in the 1960s, the height of the protests over the Vietnam War. There's that celebrated interchange between President Nixon and Dan Rather. Probably made Dan Rather's career when the president asked Rather if he was running for something, and Rather's retort: "No, Mr. President, are you?" These were clearly not years in which the press corps, certainly the White House press corps and the administration itself, had cordial relations or open lines of communication, and yet when we look at the biographies or political histories of earlier presidential administrations we learn that there was always an effort to manipulate, even intimidate, the press. Evidently, President Franklin Roosevelt's White House was quite adroit at this, threatening credentials, making clear to reporters that if they reported something the White House was unhappy with they would find themselves stopped at the gate.

Didion: But it did not have the cowing effect that it seems to have now.

Bernstein: Do you think that has something to do, again, with these business pressures of essentially these firms the reporters now represent?

Didion: I think it could. I don't know. I think what it has to do with in a real way, too, is these reporters, ever since Woodward/Bernstein, want to be inside. Now, in fact, Woodward and Bernstein at the time they did Watergate were not insiders. They were metro reporters, scrappy kids, with no inside at all. That's how they did it. But then they became stars and they became insiders as a result of Watergate. And a lot of people coming into journalism saw that and got the stardom part.

Bernstein: So they become victimized by their own success?

Didion: Yeah, and they like that sense of being inside. And they're flattered by one-on-one talks with the candidate.

Bernstein: You're fairly critical of some colleagues in the journalism field, Woodward included, in one of your essays, especially surrounding the Lewinsky scandals that plagued the Clinton administration. And Michael Isikoff at the *Washington Post* feels the sharp wit of your pen. Now, there used to be an expectation that working journalists, if not through their formal training in a journalism program, then certainly through their experience as cub reporters, you know, making their way up, would learn about the ethics of their trade. And there was some commitment to the notion that they were first and foremost public servants because they were out there to collect objective information.

Didion: Because they were out there to find out what's happening.

Bernstein: And to get it verified, and so forth. You don't speak directly to this in your essays, but you seem to be making general statements about, well, call it what it is, the decline of journalism as a professional enterprise.
Didion: Yeah, it declined as a professional enterprise, it seemed to me, even as it declined into professionalism. I don't think you have to go to journalism school. You can learn how to write a news story in about an hour and a half by writing one. Then somebody edits and it and then you know how to do it. Who, what, when, where, why, how. There's a kind of mumbo jumbo now, and what has gotten lost is any deep commitment to seeing what's happening that isn't what a source told you. A commitment to being outside the story.

Bernstein: But for many years, at least through most of the twentieth century, and then with growing regulation of media in the wake of World War II, there had been an effort to sort of erect firewalls between the journalist or news-gathering enterprise in a television station or at a newspaper or a radio station and the commercial side of the enterprise, but now it seems that firewalls have been removed. These things are conflated. We speak of "infotainment" rather than of news.
Didion: I think that's very pronounced in a lot of television.

Bernstein: Not to mention you often get the problem then of the same corporate entity that's producing the news has published Dinesh D'Souza or some pundit, so they're going to frame that work in a particular way rather than report the facts.
Didion: Yeah. The firewalls are still there in the obvious ways. Look what happened at the *Los Angeles Times* after the Staples Center—you may not have followed this but the then-publisher of the *Los Angeles Times* and his second in command decided to sell and did a package deal with the Staples Center and it included a lot of coverage, right. And this was not known to the editorial staff, and it led eventually to the publisher being let go by the Chandlers. And eventually it led, I suppose, to the sale of the paper and et cetera. But that's a very obvious kind of crossing the line. It happens all the time in more subtle ways, I think.

Bernstein: And in ways that are in invisible to *us*, the reading public. Speaking of political fictions, let's talk about another one, Newt Gingrich. You have a wonderful chapter, "Newt Gingrich, Superstar." Among historians,

we have noted, ruefully, that he received a PhD in our discipline from Tulane University, so there's no telling what damage a PhD in our discipline can do.
Didion: Have you ever watched his videos? They're astonishing.

Bernstein: They're astonishing, yes. That's a polite word. As I recall, he taught video courses. He evidently wrote a dissertation on, I believe it was on Belgian imperialism in Africa and how it was a benefit to the people of Africa.
Didion: That's right. I have a copy of this.

Bernstein: Again, you're singling him out for dissection in that chapter.
Didion: At the time I did that piece, he was still very much with us.

Bernstein: He was sort of like a meteor. He shot across the sky, then disappeared. Here he was, the speaker of the house and would foment the revolution—the Contract with America.
Didion: He was interesting in that everything that drove him, the Contract with America, we still have the fallout from that.

Bernstein: You describe him in this chapter as, "A leading beneficiary of the nation's cultural and historical amnesia." Can you talk a little bit about that?
Didion: I can't even think on how many levels he benefited from this, but the obvious one is everything he said had no relation to anything. He had no concept of history. It was kind of astonishing.

Bernstein: No facts.
Didion: No facts. What he had was principles. It was like Ten Ways to More Effective Leadership or something like that. And in fact, effective leadership was one of his principles. They were always numbered. You had five pillars of wisdom, five pillars of American history, and then if you actually tried to track them through you would find yourself lost because he himself would lose track.

Bernstein: And there's also the irony that, yes, in much of his writings and some of his videos, he talked about the importance of leadership as an historical force. He certainly subscribed to a kind of big-person theory of American history and its virtues. And yet he proved himself to be one of the most ineffective speakers in the history of the Congress. He couldn't get a laundry list passed through the Congress. So how do we account then for the fact that at the time of his ascendency—of course he's gone from the scene now, lord knows where he is—there seemed to be very little genuine criticism of these weakness or incongruities and what he had to say.

Didion: No. And I'm not sure anybody read him or listened or watched. It was astonishing. He was taken at his own face value. The way he thought of himself was as a revolutionary, a new Republican revolutionary. And that was pretty much how he was received by the press.

Bernstein: Do you think there's been an asymmetry in the way Republican leaders like Newt Gingrich in his day as speaker of the house have been treated in public by the press and by commentators and Democrats? This has a common complaint from the Democratic Party that they're not being treated with the same standards that evidently a Teflon president like Reagan or Newt Gingrich was treated in their day. Or do you think that's just whining?

Didion: I think to some extent most reporters are Democrats. It's just the way things are. And I think they are particularly and sort of reflexively careful about giving a break to the other side. I also don't think they understand Republicans. They don't seem to understand the way they talk. I'm astonished by the way I read about what George Bush has said. For example, one of the things he said in the United Nations speech was "We will have allies, we will have people at our side, etc." And this was interpreted as meaning that he had softened his position and he was not going to make a move until he had the U.N. on his side. That's not what he meant at all. Who defines the allies? He does. So he's got Tony Blair. That's the ally. It's a very common way of talking among people in business.

Bernstein: He was just utilizing the same vocabulary, now brought to the high political realm. That's an interesting argument you raise about the inability of what is arguably a Democratically inclined, in the sense of party politics, press, and the difficulties in interpreting a Republican leadership. You have rather unique credentials in this regard, and I can't resist asking you—you make clear in the book that your roots are Republican roots, you grew up in northern California in a Republican household, you've described yourself as an ardent supporter of Barry Goldwater, who certainly by today's current standards appears to be a giant among the political leaders. Full disclosure: I was raised in a Democratic Party household. Franklin Roosevelt was God, Robert Taft was the devil, and so on.

Didion: Just the opposite, you see.

Bernstein: Right. I was taught Republicans are fat and happy, you know. Now you clearly are neither. [*Laughter*] So the question is how do you account for this rather special personal odyssey, political odyssey, where you have a clear understanding of Republican roots, history—that animates much of your discussion in these essays—and yet you're very critical of the party.

Didion: Well, I think the party went in a whole other direction. I think the Republican Party doesn't bear any relationship to the Republican Party of my childhood, which was basically, at least for California Republicans, "Stay out of my life." It was small government, to keep the government out of your life. Obviously that's not what the Republican Party stands for anymore.

Bernstein: I was about to say, yes, keep government at bay, but also relatively quiet on social and cultural issues.

Didion: Totally quiet. They're private matters. I don't remember the Republican Party having any of those social issues that now dominate it.

Bernstein: We have to talk about the Lewinsky scandal.

Didion: Speaking of social issues.

Bernstein: Speaking of social and cultural issues. You have a remarkable chapter in the book, which you wonderfully title "Vichy Washington." And you talk about not only the scandal itself involving President Clinton and how this undercut his administration but also in particular how the press handled the scandal, how the political insiders who are your core subject in this volume handled the scandal. Do you think this was really an attempt at a kind of coup?

Didion: I think it was, yeah. Everybody jumped on Hillary Clinton when she said it was a vast right-wing conspiracy. Maybe it wasn't vast and maybe *conspiracy* is the wrong word, but there had been an attempt to get Clinton by the right-wing from the day he was elected. The question of impeachment didn't by any means come up when it finally happened with Monica Lewinsky. It had come up practically, again, from the inauguration. There were people giving speeches about the necessity for impeachment and the ground for which he could be impeached. This is one of those mysteries in life. Some people get hated a lot. Roosevelt did. He incited that. And Clinton for some reason was one of those polarizing personalities. So I think there was the idea of using the legal system to basically entrap him here. I saw it as an entrapment case.

Bernstein: Well, you make clear throughout the chapter—you constantly refer back to all of the available data—that the public was either unconcerned by the scandal, felt it was a diversion to invest so much time and energy in it, felt it was unfair, felt it was none of their business, any combination. And certainly felt that none of the issues that were raised in the so-called scandal addressed the leading political concerns in their own lives: health care, education, and so forth. And yet, the political handlers in Washington, your insiders, and journalists wouldn't let this thing go.

Didion: It was useful in that it allowed those social issues to come front and center, and those social issues are very important to what they consider their core constituency. Again, that tiny group of people who vote in primaries. So I think they saw a political usefulness there.

Bernstein: So that this scandal would then define a focus group that could be a lever in the election.

Didion: Right.

Bernstein: At the same time, the scandal seemed to frame some genuine areas of contestation between the major parties up on the hill. I mean the whole debate about reproductive choice, about the role of women in American society, families, gay rights, and so forth always seemed to be lurking in the background and certainly seemed to galvanize the major protagonists in this debate between the Clinton White House and the Republican leadership determined to impeach him. That debate was never joined. These things were never made vivid.

Didion: I remember it was kind of seized on by people like Robert Bork as the means by which the country would be cleansed or morally rearmed. The notion of moral rearmament was very much with us that year. William Bennett was talking about it.

Bernstein: He always talks about it.

Didion: Yeah. Bork thought there were four things that could possibly save America from itself. One was a spiritual rebirth, which you could presumably get through casting out Monica Lewinsky and the errant president. Or a war. Or economic depression.

Bernstein: This would be cleansing.

Didion: Cleansing, yes. And could rearm America.

Bernstein: And it's interesting, you go on in your final chapter to show how these themes of moral rearmament, the need to sort of cleanse the filth out of the Oval Office and so forth, that this carried onward into the presidential campaign, where Al Gore—

Didion: And it crippled it, yes.

Bernstein: He felt possessed to seize upon Joe Lieberman as his moral compass to sort of demonstrate to the American people that the Democratic Party could be a party of virtue.

Didion: Could be just as virtuous as . . . It was a nutty campaign. His own party picked on him every single time he went away from it. If you remember, right after Labor Day he raised some populist issues and was accused of throwing away the election on this ground.

Bernstein: But do you think, given the scandals that surrounded the election and the whole problem with the Florida vote, there are some—now they may very well be part of the insider class who are your target in these essays—but there are some who argue the Democratic strategy worked, but the election was stolen from them. That Gore and Lieberman actually did win Florida.

Didion: It shouldn't have been that close, though. There was no reason for it to be that close. And it was.

Bernstein: Right. It couldn't have been that effective a strategy if it left it as so fine an issue. Let me take a few minutes to talk to you actually about your career as a writer. We're a reading public here. We're fascinated and we adore all writers. And I think everyone is always curious about how writers go about their business. How do you do it? Literally, how do you find the focus? How do you find the discipline? How do you frame your days when you're engrossed in a work like this?

Didion: Well, I mean, until you do find the focus it's just really, really hard work and very dispiriting. For example, one of those pieces, what became the piece about compassionate conservatism and the moral stuff about the Bush-Gore campaign—I started out I was going to examine the Bush foreign policy, what the people around Bush during the campaign thought in terms of foreign policy. So I read through all these papers by Condoleezza Rice. There was some interesting stuff, but it seemed unlikely at that moment that it was all going to come together as a cohesive foreign policy. There was nothing, by the way, about preemptive strikes. In fact, in some places, a couple of them were talking about lifting the embargo on Cuba. You couldn't think that that was really going to happen, but maybe, you know. So while I was going through all this stuff, Bob Silvers at the *New York Review* had sent me a bunch of other books. He sent me this book by Marvin Olasky and I started reading it, so then I got more interested in that and started talking about compassionate conservatism. So it takes a long time to focus in.

Bernstein: Once you do engage with material, when you mark out your terrain, is it your practice to sort of write in a white heat, just start and keep going till you're done? Or is it a sort of day-by-day, bit-by-bit process? Or is it not predictable at all?

Didion: No, it's day-by-day, bit-by-bit because the whole meaning of anything for me is in the grammar. It doesn't mean anything until I've written it. I don't have a lot of thoughts. They don't form until I've written it down. So the process of writing is the process of thinking.

Bernstein: What's always very clear in your essays is there's always clearly a lot of preparation. I mean, you're doing a lot of homework. I know that several of your reviewers have said that recently about this very book and some of the other essay work that led to it. They said, "This is astonishing. Here's a writer who's actually read Dinesh D'Souza, Newt Gingrich, and the rest of them, page for page."

Didion: Isn't that surprising that that's surprising?

Bernstein: Well, it sort of goes back to this whole discussion of just what journalists and others are up to. They pontificate on an array of issues, but they clearly haven't done the homework, the preparation to speak with precision about some of these issues.

Didion: You know, I was an English major at Berkeley, and it was during the time they were doing New Criticism there. So I learned all that backwards and forwards, all that close textual analysis.

Bernstein: And don't talk about the context at all.

Didion: So I still go to the text.

Bernstein: Well, we have a few minutes left. None of us can avoid the opportunity of asking a contemporary political analyst about the current situation and what weighs heavily on everyone's minds about the possibility of war overseas, what the current administration is up to. And to the extent that you are connected in this world of political analysts and commentators, do you think it's fair to regard the posturing of the Bush administration in the last few weeks as a kind of waging-the-dog syndrome? Is the president simply trying to reap domestic benefits out of a foreign policy adventure?

Didion: I don't think it's as straightforward as that, but I think that certainly there's an element there. And then with Al-Qaeda, who knows where we are in that? We're not where the president said we would be. And I can't avoid thinking there's an element of pulling down a new scrim.

Bernstein: A new slate, sort of like an Etch A Sketch, you shake it and it goes blank.

Didion: Yeah. There are a lot of things at work here. What they all add up to feels like the days before World War I. It has that kind of inexorable drift toward—

Bernstein: It's interesting that you choose World War I as an example since, at least in the days leading up to the start of that war, but ultimately US involvement in that war, there didn't seem to be a lot of discussion about war aims. Unlike World War II, for example. The record shows the Roosevelt administration went to great lengths to firmly articulate goals and strategies. But there doesn't seem to be much discussion of—we hear this phrase "regime change."

Didion: Regime change, yes, but to what? And immediately if you question regime change you hear "weapons of mass destruction." The attempt to make the case was not an argued case. It was just a repetition of those phrases.

Bernstein: And you've also just offered the very interesting observation about Al-Qaeda, where we are in this effort. Where do we want to be?

Didion: Well, where the president wanted to be was "Dead or Alive," right? That's not the case. It was badly defined. It was very popular at the moment he said it. It fit the mood of the country in a way, probably. But it was always a wrong definition because we weren't talking about one man ever. We were talking about something else. If you got rid of one man you were not going to get rid of the problem. You still hear people in the administration talking about "terrorism" as if it were some kind of freak of nature that just sprang up out of nowhere, right, and not a political technique or tactic, and not usually coming into play in a context. And if you tried to say something like that, it was written off in the early days as not patriotic. Susan Sontag got very beaten up for saying that this had a context, right? Later, the response was a little more nuanced, but it was the same thing. You, the speaker, had been taken in.

Bernstein: You'd been duped.
Didion: You'd been duped, yeah, as a typical liberal.

Notes

1. This adaptation of Hemingway's short story was part of an HBO film called *Women and Men: Stories of Seduction* (1990).

Dave Eggers Talks with Joan Didion

Dave Eggers / 2003

From *The Believer Book of Writers Talking to Writers* (McSweeney's). © 2008 by Dave Eggers. Reprinted by permission.

"I'm invisible Scarlet O'Neil in Washington. I mean, it doesn't have any currency. Being Joan Didion means nothing."

Unfortunate decisions California citizens have made:
Electing two movie-star governors
Building prisons to create jobs
Neglecting the public school system in favor of short-term gains
Committing a lot of sane people to mental institutions

This interview took place in San Francisco, in the fall of 2003, as part of a series of onstage interviews presented by City Arts & Lectures. The venue was the Herbst Theatre, which seats about nine hundred. Didion had done interviews at the Herbst before, and while watching her previous event[s], I'd learned that she seemed to prefer to chat than to be asked to expound. Ponderous, open-ended questions—"Why do you write, Ms. Didion?"—were not going to work. So on this night I tried to keep the mood buoyant and conversational, especially given that the subject matter of her then-latest book, Where I Was From, *was not sunny.*

That book, by the way, is no less brilliant than The White Album *and* Slouching Towards Bethlehem, *the collections of her pieces—part journalism, part cultural critique, part memoir—that established her as a writer of uncommon acuity and a voice that spoke to and about a certain generation at a critical point. Like those early books,* Where I Was From *showcases her perfectly calibrated style, and like all of her recent work, including* Political Fictions, *it has lost nothing on her reputation-making books of the late sixties and seventies. As always, her prose is both precise and fluid, cruelly accurate while often revealing the vulnerabilities of its author.*

Didion has, of course, written great novels too, and has said that each time she starts writing a novel, she re-reads Joseph Conrad's Victory. *Though the style of that book is a bit more rococo than Didion's minimalist prose, it's evident why it would seem to inspire books like* The Last Thing He Wanted *and* A Book of Common Prayer. Victory *concerns intrigue among travelers in the islands of the Far East, a cast of misfits, of whom most are wanderers, abandoners. They leave husbands, children, their countries, and they get involved in very tricky business. These are the characters that populate Didion's fiction, and her heroines are among the most complex, even opaque, in contemporary fiction.*

Because Didion's prose is so extraordinarily sharp, some expect that in person Didion would be a kind of raconteur, a spewer of devastating bon mots. But she's far more personable than that. She is a person, actually, very much a person, even though her name now has about it the sound of legend. The Legend of Joan Didion—that could be a western, or a book by James Fenimore Cooper. "The Ballad of Joan Didion"—maybe a song by Bob Dylan? It means so much, that name, Joan Didion, even if she denies it.

Dave Eggers: So we're going to just get started. I have the questions printed on blue cards.
Joan Didion: It's beautiful type, too. [*Laughter*]

DE: That means they're going to be good. [*Laughter*] So we met about six or seven years ago when I interviewed you for *Salon*.
JD: Yes. And I didn't even—I wasn't on the net at the time. And I did not know what *Salon* was. As a matter of fact, I wanted to cancel the interview because I had so many things to do and I thought, "What is this? Why am I doing this?" [*Laughter*]

DE: Yeah, and there were many years after that when people were still wondering. [*Laughter*]
JD: That was 1996. It was only seven years ago.

DE: At the time, one of my favorite answers that you gave was when I asked what you missed about California. Do you remember what you said?
JD: No.

DE: Driving. You talked about how you missed that uninterrupted line of thought that you had when you drove.[1] And you've written about it, about L.A.

JD: My husband and I moved to New York in 1988, and to negotiate going to the grocery store meant you had to go out on the street and deal with a lot of *people*, you know? You had to maybe run into a neighbor—certainly run into somebody in the elevator, run into a doorman. It took you out of your whole train of thought. Whereas if you walked out of your driveway and got in your car and went to the store, not a soul was going to enter your mind-stream. You could just continue kind of focusing on what you were doing.

DE: You still have a California driver's license.

JD: I do.

DE: With a New York address on it.

JD: Yes, it does. Mm-hm. [*Laughs*] You know how I got it?

DE: No. How would that work?

JD: Well, my mother was living in Monterey and I was visiting her. I had to renew my license, so I went up to—I think it was Oceanside. And I said, "Uh, you know I'm not *actually* living in California right now; I'm living in New York. Can I put that address on?" She said, "Put wherever you want us to send it." [*Laughs*]

DE: And another thing, when we talked then, we talked about a book called *Holy Land*, written by D. J. Waldie, about Lakewood, California. And then, shortly around that time you wrote about Lakewood yourself, and that would become the first piece—

JD: Part of *Where I Was From*. And in fact, when I wrote about Lakewood, it was 1993. It was a piece for the *New Yorker*—Tina Brown was then the editor and she was interested in this. When I said I wanted to do Lakewood, she was crazy for me to do Lakewood because there was this group of high-school boys called the Spur Posse who were all over shows like *Montel* at the time. They did this totally predictable and not very unusual thing for high-school boys. They kept a point system on girls they had slept with, right? And for this, this somehow gained them all this notoriety. But anyway, what interested me about Lakewood was that it was a defense-industry town. And it was during the middle of the defense cut-backs, and so I thought that would be an interesting thing to do. And I met

D. J. Waldie then, and he was doing this series of pieces—not *pieces*, they were pieces of a *novel*, it turned out—which he was publishing in literary magazines. And he gave them to me and I was just *stunned*—I mean, they were so good.

DE: *Holy Land* is an incredible book. And the Lakewood section is one of the primary elements in *Where I Was From*.
JD: Well, what happened is, I finished that piece, and I realized that, even though it was eighteen thousand words long or whatever—I mean, it didn't run that long in the *New Yorker,* but that's how long I'd written it—that I hadn't *answered* the questions I had. That it'd raised more questions about California than I'd answered. I hadn't even thought of it as about California when I started it; I thought of it as about the defense industry, right? The kind of withering of the defense industry in Southern California. But then it turned out to raise some kind of deeper questions about what California was about. So then I started doing some more reading and started play-ing around with the idea of doing—of trying to answer those other ques-tions about what California was about. And finally—I didn't realize—it was only quite late, when I was writing the book, that I realized that was what Lakewood was about. The person who would explain what Lakewood was, was Henry George, who had written this before the Southern Pacific, when everybody in California was excited about the glories the railroad would bring. He wrote this piece—it was the first piece he ever wrote—for the *Overland Monthly* called "What the Railroad Will Bring Us." And Lakewood was really an answer to what the railroad had brought us. I mean, it was the answer to what the ideal . . . It's too complicated. [*Laughter*]

DE: Lakewood was like a Levittown. And it was supposed to be bigger than that, and it went up overnight and all the houses were identical.
JD: They all went on sale the same day. It was bigger than the original Levittown, actually. And it was designed around a regional shopping center. If you look at the *Thomas Guide* book—this is what got me excited about it—to this day, you see the shopping center in the middle of town. You see a public golf course, nine holes, over on the corner of the town. And then down below, you see the Douglas plant. This is a kind of really simple town. And the houses were all identical. I mean, I think there were something like eight basic models, but they were all pretty much alike. They came in various colors and you couldn't have two of the same color next door to each other.

DE: They had a choice of colors and models—

JD: Yeah, but you had to rotate them on a block. And they were really quite small. They were two-and three-bedrooms, but they were nine hundred and fifty to eleven hundred square feet, which is—I mean, I've lived in apartments which were eight-hundred-and-fifty square feet, and it's not a lot of, you know, space. For a three-bedroom house.

DE: But the piece about Lakewood crystallized a lot of the issues that you've been writing about.

JD: *Opened* a lot of the issues. Yeah. I mean, really, it raised all these questions. That's why I started writing this.

DE: So in this book—you've been writing about California for so long, but never with such, I think, *finality*. You know, you really come to conclusions here. Basically, you mentioned the Southern Pacific Railroad and how California has this history of selling itself out for the short gain—you know, short-sightedly—selling its land to the Southern Pacific Railroad, for example. And in some ways, your book is fantastic, because California hasn't changed that much in its shortsightedness. Can you talk about that, about the process of realizing that the state has always sort of been this way?

JD: Well, all these things kept happening. I kept thinking that this was evidence of how California had changed. I mean, one of the things that really deeply shocked me was when I realized that California no longer had a really functioning public school system. That its scores were now on a par with *Mississippi's*. And that the University of California system was no longer *valued* as it had been. And that the investment at the state level was not being made there. And yet, we were building all these new prisons. I thought this was evidence of how California had changed, but it wasn't. I mean, I finally realized it was the same deal. It was selling the future, selling the state, in return for someone's agreement—short-term agreement—to enrich us. People want prisons in their town because they think it'll bring jobs, right? Well, it doesn't even bring jobs, and what does it bring for the future?

DE: But now everything's changed. We had a recall, and we have a new governor, he was an action star—I think we've been really far-sighted about that, at least. [*Laughter*] So you must be thinking optimistically, now. Finally there's a break, and we're thinking of the future—looking ahead. [*Laughter*] But you commented on Arnold's election somewhere, I think. I didn't see it firsthand, but didn't you say, "Nothing good can come of this."? [*Laughter*]

JD: I probably did. [*Laughter*] I was so sort of thrilled over the weekend: I saw in the *Los Angeles Times* that part of the way the budget had been balanced by Gray Davis included getting rid of a huge number of state jobs. But as things progressed, he didn't—Gray Davis didn't—have a chance to get rid of those people. I mean, he could do it now, but he's not going to. And so it will fall to Arnold Schwarzenegger, who will have to make a decision: either to follow through on the job cuts or to find that money someplace else. Where will that money come from? And he keeps talking about bringing *new business* in. Where is this new business coming from?

DE: Well, it was interesting: you talk about how California has this history of individualism and self-reliance, but from the beginning the state has depended pretty heavily on federal money.
JD: Yeah.

DE: And here, Bush came to the state, and Arnold was crowing about how George will come back and give us some money and he'll bail us out. He called himself the Collectinator.
JD: And he himself was deeply into that individual effort, yes. He's almost an exemplar of the kind of error that we've seen over the years in California. [*Laughter*]

DE: Well, the whole map is right here in your book, the blueprint for how this state is run. It's amazing that—well, I don't know. If everybody had read this, I think we might have had a different result with the whole recall effort. It's all there.

Let's back up a little bit and talk about the writing of your book. California has always been a very personal subject for you, and you've woven together the state itself and your upbringing here. And at the same time, this book is sort of about the loss of a certain California that you knew.
JD: Yeah, well, I don't think I could have written it before my parents died. I don't mean that we would have had a fight about it—we wouldn't have had a fight about it at all. But I just couldn't have done it, because it was not their idea. That's one thing. The other thing is that the death of my parents started me thinking more about what my own relationship to California was. Because it kind of threw it up for grabs. You know, when your parents die, you're not exactly *from* the place you were from. I don't know, it's just an odd—it's an odd thing.

DE: Early in the book you trace the paths of many of your ancestors in coming to California. And it connects a lot with the heroines in many of your novels. I think you find sort of the DNA for them in the passage that describes many of your—[*DE gives JD the passage in question*]

JD: Everybody in my family moved on the frontier. I mean, they moved on the frontier, through several centuries. Wherever the frontier was, that's where they were. [*Reading*]

> These women in my family would seem to have been pragmatic and in their deepest instincts clinically radical, given to breaking clean with everyone and everything they knew. They could shoot and they could handle stock and when their children outgrew their shoes they could learn from the Indians how to make moccasins. "An old lady in our wagon train taught my sister to make blood pudding," Narcissa Cornwall recalled. "After killing a deer or steer you cut its throat and catch the blood. You add suet to this and a little salt, and meal or flour if you have it, and bake it. If you haven't anything else to eat, it's pretty good." They tended to accommodate any means in pursuit of an uncertain end. They tended to avoid dwelling on just what that end might imply. When they could not think what else to do they moved another thousand miles, set out another garden: beans and squash and sweet peas from seeds carried from the last place. The past could be jettisoned, children buried and parents left behind, but seeds got carried.

DE: And when we spoke many years ago we talked about connections between the heroines in *A Book of Common Prayer* and *Run River*, and that passage connected a lot of them together, these women that were—

JD: Even the woman in the last novel—Elena McMahon, in *The Last Thing He Wanted*—she was similar in some ways.

DE: Right. When you were writing *Where I Was From*, did you realize the connections between all those characters in your novels, that their DNA was that of the frontier women in your family's history?

JD: No. No. No. I didn't.

DE: So we just, right now, we just did it. We just figured it out. [*Laughter*] Wow, that was good. That was easy. [*Laughter*] But so there's this idea of "I'm debunking the myth of California" that runs throughout the book, and in many different ways. But you've also said that you see this book as sort of a love letter to California. Can you explain that?

JD: Well, you don't bother getting mad at people you don't love, right? I mean, you just, you don't. I mean, why would I spend all that time trying to figure it out if I didn't have a feeling for it?

DE: There's a passage near the end, when you're driving from Monterey to Berkeley and your mother's asking, "Are we on the right road? This doesn't look familiar, are we on the right road?" And you keep reassuring her that you're on 101 North, that this is the correct road. And then she finally says, "Then where did it all go?"
JD: Mm-hm.

DE: And there's also a passage, way back, from *Slouching Towards Bethlehem* that went, "All that is constant about the California of my childhood is the rate at which it disappears."
JD: Yeah. Well, at the time I wrote that line, very little of it had disappeared compared with the amount that has disappeared now. I think I was thinking specifically about the *one subdivision* that had been built that was visible from the road between Sacramento and Berkeley. Well, now it's a little bit more built up than that. [*Laughter*] What Mother was talking about when we were driving up from Monterey, that had happened just in a few years. I mean, suddenly, suddenly, suddenly everything had disappeared—suddenly all the open space on 101 south of San Jose was gone. I mean, it had been gone north of San Jose for some time. First Morgan Hill went. Then Gilroy went. Salinas may be next. We were just north of Salinas when Mother was so troubled.

DE: There's a man that you cite in one of the pieces, Lincoln Steffens, who talks about deep ecology, the belief that humans are inevitably going to destroy themselves, and so we shouldn't worry so much about things like recycling. Are you fatalistic about the future of California?
JD: Well, you know, if you extrapolated from the history, you would not be optimistic. But I keep thinking that we're all capable of learning, you know? That somehow we will, we will see—we'll realize the value of what we have and actually make a commitment to invest in the university, keep some open land, you know, just some basic things.

DE: Switching back: Tonight, Michael Moore is speaking at San Francisco State, and you and I talked a little bit before about the political climate right now. You've always been—to I'm sure everyone here—an exemplar of someone who can find nuance and who doesn't necessarily look for the black and the white and the easy answers in your political writing. But right now we're at a point where there is a shrillness to the debate. You turn on the TV and find MSNBC and Chris Matthews and everything else, all so loud and abusive. What's your political diet? What do you watch? What do you read?

JD: Oh, I read a lot. You know, I get five newspapers. But in order to follow what's going on, you actually have to look at television at certain points, because otherwise you don't realize how *toxic* it's become. You get no sense of the confrontational level of everything. I don't know what it is. The obvious answer is it's 24/7 television, it's cable. But how cable took the form of people shouting at each other, I don't know.

DE: In a way, it's a positive thing that Michael Moore is being read so widely, and that Al Franken has a number one book. But then these books keep reacting to each other. I don't know when it's going to end. And I don't know who's *buying all of the books*—

JD: But somebody is. There's a secret there. Ann Coulter's book, for example—is she the *Treason* or the *Liar* one? I can't—

DE: There's a *lie* somewhere in there.

JD: Yeah.

DE: And her face on the cover, which is nice.

JD: It has a little—there's a little code icon next to it on the bestseller list in the *New York Times,* which indicates that a lot of its sales have been in bulk. [*Laughter*]

DE: Oh, that's true.

JD: And so that's where some of it's coming from. But who the bulk is, I don't—[*Laughter*]

DE: No, that's how it works. But now, *Fixed Ideas,* which is your short book that *New York Review Books* put out, begins on the stage we're sitting on, when you were here in 2001, in September.

JD: Yeah, it was just after. It was like a week after the event.

DE: Right, and it talks about you touring in the weeks after 9/11 and fearing the quality of discourse. And the people that you met along the road were all afraid of the inability to speak out after that and—

JD: I don't know if they were afraid. They were speaking out, they were absolutely speaking out. I mean, I was amazed. I had sort of arrived from New York like a zombie to do this book tour, which seemed like the least relevant thing anybody could possibly be doing, and to my amazement, every place I went people were making connections between our political life—which is what the book was—I was promoting *Political Fictions.* There are many connections between our political life and what happened on September 11. Connections I hadn't even thought to make. I was still so numb. And so then I got back to New York after two weeks, and I discovered that everybody had stopped talking in New York. I mean it was—everybody had flags out instead. And the *New York Times* was running "Portraits of Grief," which were these little sentimental stories about—little vignettes about the dead. I mean it was kind of—it was a scary, scary thing.

DE: In *Fixed Ideas,* you wrote that the people you spoke to recognized that "even then, with flames still visible in lower Manhattan . . . the words 'bipartisanship' and 'national unity' had come to mean acquiescence to the administration's pre-existing agenda—for example, the imperative for further tax cuts, the necessity for Arctic drilling, the systemic elimination of regulatory and union protections, even the funding for the missile shield." Do you feel that the quality of debate has gotten better since then?
JD: No. I mean, the president is still using—is now using September 11 when he's asked about *campaign funding.* [*Laughter*] No, it's true. He was asked why it was necessary for him to raise *x* million dollars, or whatever it was, for his primary campaign when he was unopposed, and he said that he remembered the way this country was, that he'll never forget September 11. [*Laughter*] And that it was important for him to remain in office, too. [*Laughter*]

DE: Do you have plans to cover the next campaign?
JD: I don't have any plans to cover it. No, I just don't have the heart to cover it. I mean, I might read about it and then write about it, but I'm not going to get on those planes now. [*Laughter*]

DE: No?
JD: No.

DE: Was there a point in your career when being Joan Didion got in the way of your being a reporter? When you couldn't hide anymore, you couldn't just observe?

JD: I think I can usually hide. Especially around politics. I'm Invisible Scarlet O'Neil in Washington. I mean, it doesn't have any currency. Being Joan Didion means nothing. [*Laughs*]

DE: There's a great passage in *The White Album*, in a piece you were doing about Nancy Reagan. And who was that for? And why?
JD: I had a column every other week for the *Saturday Evening Post*, a magazine that no longer exists. So I decided to go to Sacramento, to interview Nancy Reagan, who had become the governor's wife.

DE: And there was a camera crew there, and you were there, and there was a lot of discussion of how to make her seem like she was having a normal day.
JD: Yeah, the camera crew was there to see what she was doing on an ordinary Tuesday morning in Sacramento. This was, like, her first year in Sacramento. And I was there to see what she was doing on an ordinary Tuesday morning in Sacramento. [*Laughs*] So we were all kind of watching each other. And then she said, "I might be picking . . . I might be picking . . ." and the cameraman asked her if she might be picking roses. And she said, "I might be *picking* them, but I won't be *using* them!" [*Laughter*]

DE: I never got that part. Did you get it? I never understood what that meant?
JD: It was just—she wasn't having a dinner party. She didn't have dinner parties in Sacramento. She only had them in the *Pacific Palisades,* so she wouldn't be *using* the flowers. I think that's what *she* meant, but what I heard was, it was, you know, sort of a bad actress's line. [*Laughter*] More animation than was required.

DE: You wrote about a trip with Bush Sr., when he was vice president, going to Israel and Jordan. They would always have to have the right backdrop. In Jordan, Bush's people made sure that there was an American flag in every frame, and a *camel*.
JD: A camel. [*Laughter*] I guess that was to clarify the setting, you know?

DE: And at one point they said they wanted Bush to be looking through binoculars at enemy territory. Who knows why. So they give him a pair of binoculars, and then they realized the direction he was looking was Israel.

[*Laughter*] When you were following Dukakis, and when they had him play-ing ball, you wrote that it was "insider baseball." That was also a title of one of the pieces.

JD: "Insider baseball," yeah. It was astonishing.

DE: Yeah. Because they wanted to make them seem real, so everywhere they would go, Dukakis and one of his guys would play baseball—play catch outside the airplane.

JD: On the tarmac, yeah.

DE: And then you would be invited to watch—

JD: Right, and then if anybody missed it—I don't mean if *I* missed it, I could have missed it and they wouldn't have even noticed, but if one of the *net-works* missed it, they wanted everybody to film it, right—if anybody missed it, they would do it again. [*Laughter*]

DE: And why does everybody—you're astonished by it when you're cover-ing these campaigns, but everybody goes along with the same sort of events. "OK, now we're going to go out, and the candidate is going to eat broccoli, and that's going to lead the next day's news." But everybody goes along with it. They're trading access; they want the access and then in exchange, the campaign gives them this moment.

JD: Yes. You don't want to get thrown off the campaign. That's the key thing about covering a campaign, for people who cover them, is you can't—

DE: You don't want to get thrown off the plane.

JD: Right. You want to be there. So it's a trade for access. In case something happens, right? But nothing is going to happen—

DE: Well, somebody's going to fall off a platform one of these days, right?

JD: Somebody did, remember?

DE: That was Dole.

JD: Yeah, in Chico.

DE: OK. Now we're going to do a quick speed round. With these questions, you're allowed to answer only *yes* or *no*. [*Laughter*] OK, here we go. Will there be another recall, this one of Arnold?

JD: No.

DE: Should there be one?
JD: No, I don't believe in recalls.

DE: Just yes or no, please. [*Laughter*] Will you ever move back to California?
JD: I can't answer that *yes* or *no*. [*Laughter*]

DE: Can you believe how well this interview is going? [*Laughter*]
JD: Yes.

DE: Have you written a screenplay where you were happy with the final product?
JD: Yes.

DE: What was that? You're allowed to answer.
JD: *True Confessions*.

DE: Is that the one with—
JD: De Niro and Duvall.

DE: Oh, right. And—
JD: And it was directed by . . . I know him as well as I know my own name: Ulu Grosbard. We had a good time on it, and I was happy with it. In fact, I see it on television and it still makes me cry.

DE: So it was written by just you and your husband?
JD: Yeah. In fact, we did all the changes during shooting; we did them on the weekend. Ulu would come over—we were shooting in Los Angeles and he would come over and we would make the changes while he sat there on Sunday afternoon. It was really easy.

DE: So you were on set the whole time?
JD: No, we weren't on set. We were at a house in Brentwood. [*Laughs*] But Sundays they had off, so he would come over on Sunday and we would do it.

DE: OK, a few more in the speed round. Can Wes Clark beat George Bush?
JD: If he were nominated, yeah.

DE: Can Howard Dean beat George Bush?
JD: I doubt it.

DE: And finally: really, though, can you believe how well this is going? [*Laughter*]
JD: Yes.

DE: There's a line in the new book where you say, "Not much about California, on its own preferred terms, has encouraged its children to see themselves as connected to one another." Can you explain that?
JD: People in Northern California grew up with the whole founding myth of California, the whole crossing story, et cetera. Southern California was founded on a different story. The only time when I felt, really, a big connection between Northern and Southern California—and I've lived in both—was when PSA was flying. [*Laughter*] No, I mean, literally, PSA connected the state where you could fly—

DE: Explain what PSA is.
JD: Pacific Southwest Airways. You weren't here then, probably. They had these planes with these big smiles painted on them. And you could fly from Sacramento to Los Angeles for I think sixteen dollars, and you could fly from Los Angeles to San Francisco for twelve. And there was what they called a Midnight Flyer, so you could fly up for dinner, in San Francisco, and then fly home, to Los Angeles, or vice versa. I mean, it gave a great sense of mobility around the state, which has been—which we never had before, and I haven't felt it since. I mean, going from Los Angeles to San Francisco on a plane now is so unpleasant that my brother always drives—you know, he does this all the time.

DE: So you're talking about mostly regionally there, between coastal, inland, north, south.
JD: There were a lot of things I was thinking about there, I suppose. I was also thinking, the idea, the ethic that everybody kind of believed represented California, was one of extreme individualism, and we did not feel very responsible for others in the community. Community wasn't a big idea.

DE: And that's something you feel is prevalent throughout this state? Is that something grounded in the myth of California?
JD: In the way it was settled, yeah. I mean the kinds of people who settled it. The idea was, basically, California was settled by people who wanted to strike it rich, in a way, at the simplest level. And *as* individuals. This ethic kind of took hold; it became a big point of pride even though everyone in the state

was heavily dependent on federal government. We didn't feel very responsible for those around us. One of the things that really knocked me out when I was writing this book was the thing about the committal to mental hospitals in the early days of the state. And right into the early twentieth century, people were committed at a higher rate than almost anywhere else in the country. And it was explained that they were kind of unhinged by the ups and downs of life on the frontier, in the gold camps . . . This wasn't it, I don't think. It was just an extreme disregard for, and a refusal to tolerate, the people around them. I mean, people were being committed in San Francisco for—one older woman was committed by her sister. This was a study done by somebody who had gotten hold of all these records. One woman was committed by her sister because she had lost all interest in crocheting. [*Laughter*]

DE: And the national committal rate was, what, 3,900 people committed in one year. And 2,600 of them were from California, or something like that.
JD: Yeah, I mean huge, huge numbers. And they were committed basically for life. I mean, it wasn't one of those forty-eight-hour deals.

DE: We talked about a passage that I was going to ask you to read, and you asked me to read it, that I think sums up a lot of what is central—both your love of the state and then ambivalence, and also the sense of loss. After your mother died, you flew back to California, and this occurs late in the book. Do you want to read it, or should I?
JD: You read it.

DE: "Flying to Monterey I had a sharp apprehension of the many times before when I had, like Lincoln Steffens, 'come back,' flown west, followed the sun, each time experiencing a lightening of spirit as the land below opened up, the checkerboards of the Midwestern plains giving way to the vast empty reach between the Rockies and the Sierra Nevada; then *home, there, where I was from, me,* California. It would be a while before I realized that 'me' is what we think when our parents die, even at my age, *who will look out for me now, who will remember me as I was, who will know what happens to me now, where will I be from.*"

Notes

1. Neither Eggers nor *Salon* was able to find the original interview transcript that contains this discussion of driving.

Joan Didion:
The Art of Nonfiction No 1.

Hilton Als / 2006

From *The Paris Review,* Issue 176, Spring 2006. Copyright © 2006 by *The Paris Review.* Reprinted by permission of the Wylie Agency LLC.

The last time this magazine spoke with Joan Didion, in August of 1977, she was living in California and had just published her third novel, *A Book of Common Prayer.* Didion was forty-two years old and well-known not only for her fiction but also for her work in magazines—reviews, reportage, and essays—some of which had been collected in *Slouching Towards Bethlehem* (1968). In addition, Didion and her husband, John Gregory Dunne (who was himself the subject of a *Paris Review* interview in 1996), had written a number of screenplays together, including *The Panic in Needle Park* (1971); an adaptation of her second novel, *Play It As It Lays* (1972); and *A Star Is Born* (1976). When Didion's first interview appeared in these pages in 1978, she was intent on exploring her gift for fiction and nonfiction. Since then, her breadth and craft as a writer have only grown deeper with each project.

Joan Didion was born in Sacramento, and both her parents, too, were native Californians. She studied English at Berkeley, and in 1956, after graduating, she won an essay contest sponsored by *Vogue* and moved to New York City to join the magazine's editorial staff. While at *Vogue,* she wrote fashion copy, as well as book and movie reviews. She also became a frequent contributor to *The National Review,* among other publications. In 1963, Didion published her first novel, *Run River.* The next year she married Dunne, and soon afterwards, they moved to Los Angeles. There, in 196[6], they adopted their only child, Quintana Roo.

In 1973, Didion began writing for *The New York Review of Books,* where she has remained a regular contributor. While she has continued to write novels in recent decades—*Democracy* (1984) and *The Last Thing He Wanted*

(1996)—she has increasingly explored different forms of nonfiction: critical essay, political reportage, memoir. In 1979, she published a second collection of her magazine work, *The White Album*, which was followed by *Salvador* (1983), *Miami* (1987), *After Henry* (1992), *Political Fictions* (2001), and *Where I Was From* (2003). In the spring of 2005, Didion was awarded a Gold Medal from the American Academy of Arts and Letters.

In December of 2003, shortly before their fortieth anniversary, Didion's husband died. Last fall, she published *The Year of Magical Thinking*, a book-length meditation on grief and memory. It became a best-seller, and won the National Book Award for nonfiction; Didion is now adapting the book for the stage as a monologue. Two months before the book's publication, Didion's thirty-nine-year-old daughter died after a long illness.

Our conversation took place over the course of two afternoons in the Manhattan apartment Didion shared with her husband. On the walls of the spacious flat, one could see many photographs of Didion, Dunne, and their daughter. Daylight flooded the book-filled parlor. "When we got the place, we assumed the sun went all through the apartment. It doesn't," Didion said, laughing. Her laughter was the additional punctuation to her precise speech.

INTERVIEWER: By now you've written at least as much nonfiction as you have fiction. How would you describe the difference between writing the one or the other?

JOAN DIDION: Writing fiction is for me a fraught business, an occasion of daily dread for at least the first half of the novel, and sometimes all the way through. The work process is totally different from writing nonfiction. You have to sit down every day and make it up. You have no notes—or sometimes you do, I made extensive notes for *A Book of Common Prayer*—but the notes give you only the background, not the novel itself. In nonfiction, the notes give you the piece. Writing nonfiction is more like sculpture, a matter of shaping the research into the finished thing. Novels are like paintings, specifically watercolors. Every stroke you put down you have to go with. Of course you can rewrite, but the original strokes are still there in the texture of the thing.

INTERVIEWER: Do you do a lot of rewriting?

DIDION: When I'm working on a book, I constantly retype my own sentences. Every day I go back to page one and just retype what I have. It gets me into a rhythm. Once I get over maybe a hundred pages, I won't go back to page one, but I might go back to page fifty-five, or twenty, even. But then every once in a while I feel the need to go to page one again and start rewriting. At the end of the day, I mark up the pages I've done—pages or *page*—all the way back to page one. I mark them up so that I can retype them in the morning. It gets me past that blank terror.

INTERVIEWER: Did you do that sort of retyping for *The Year of Magical Thinking*?

DIDION: I did. It was especially important with this book because so much of it depended on echo. I wrote it in three months, but I marked it up every night.

INTERVIEWER: The book moves quickly. Did you think about how your readers would read it?

DIDION: Of course, you always think about how it will be read. I always aim for a reading in one sitting.

INTERVIEWER: At what point did you know that the notes you were writing in response to John's death would be a book for publication?

DIDION: John died December 30, 2003. Except for a few lines written a day or so after he died, I didn't begin making the notes that became the book until the following October. After a few days of making notes, I realized that I was thinking about how to structure a book, which was the point at which I realized that I was writing one. This realization in no way changed what I was writing.

INTERVIEWER: Was it difficult to finish the book? Or were you happy to have your life back—to live with a lower level of self-scrutiny?

DIDION: Yes. It was difficult to finish the book. I didn't want to let John go. I don't really have my life back yet, since Quintana died only on August 26.

INTERVIEWER: Since you write about yourself, interviewers tend to ask about your personal life; I want to ask you about writing and books. In the past you've written pieces on V. S. Naipaul, Graham Greene, Norman Mailer, and Ernest Hemingway—titanic, controversial iconoclasts whom you tend to defend. Were these the writers you grew up with and wanted to emulate?

DIDION: Hemingway was really early. I probably started reading him when I was just eleven or twelve. There was just something magnetic to me in the arrangement of those sentences. Because they were so simple—or rather they appeared to be so simple, but they weren't.

Something I was looking up the other day, that's been in the back of my mind, is a study done several years ago about young women's writing skills and the incidence of Alzheimer's. As it happens, the subjects were all nuns, because all of these women had been trained in a certain convent. They found that those who wrote simple sentences as young women later had a higher incidence of Alzheimer's, while those who wrote complicated sentences with several clauses had a lower incidence of Alzheimer's. The assumption—which I thought was probably erroneous—was that those who tended to write simple sentences as young women did not have strong memory skills.

INTERVIEWER: Though you wouldn't classify Hemingway's sentences as simple.

DIDION: No, they're deceptively simple because he always brings a change in.

INTERVIEWER: Did you think you could write that kind of sentence? Did you want to try?

DIDION: I didn't think that I could do them, but I thought that I could learn—because they felt so natural. I could see how they worked once I started typing them out. That was when I was about fifteen. I would just type those stories. It's a great way to get rhythms into your head.

INTERVIEWER: Did you read anyone else before Hemingway?

DIDION: No one who attracted me in that way. I had been reading a lot of plays. I had a misguided idea that I wanted to act. The form this took was not acting, however, but reading plays. Sacramento was not a place where you saw a lot of plays. I think the first play I ever saw was the Lunts in the touring company of *O Mistress Mine.* I don't think that that's what inspired me. The Theater Guild used to do plays on the radio, and I remember being very excited about listening to them. I remember memorizing speeches from *Death of a Salesman* and *Member of the Wedding* in the period right after the war.

INTERVIEWER: Which playwrights did you read?

DIDION: I remember at one point going through everything of Eugene O'Neill's. I was struck by the sheer theatricality of his plays. You could see how they worked. I read them all one summer. I had nosebleeds, and for some reason it took all summer to get the appointment to get my nose cauterized. So I just lay still on the porch all day and read Eugene O'Neill. That was all I did. And dab at my face with an ice cube.

INTERVIEWER: What you really seem to have responded to in these early influences was style—voice and form.

DIDION: Yes, but another writer I read in high school who just knocked me out was Theodore Dreiser. I read *An American Tragedy* all in one weekend and couldn't put it down—I locked myself in my room. Now that was antithetical to every other book I was reading at the time, because Dreiser really had no style, but it was powerful.

And one book I totally missed when I first read it was *Moby-Dick*. I reread it when Quintana was assigned it in high school. It was clear that she wasn't going to get through it unless we did little talks about it at dinner. I had not gotten it at all when I read it at her age. I had missed that wild control of language. What I had thought discursive were really these great leaps. The book had just seemed a jumble; I didn't get the control in it.

INTERVIEWER: After high school you wanted to go to Stanford. Why?

DIDION: It's pretty straightforward—all my friends were going to Stanford.

INTERVIEWER: But you went to Berkeley and majored in literature. What were you reading there?

DIDION: The people I did the most work on were Henry James and D. H. Lawrence, who I was not high on. He irritated me on almost every level.

INTERVIEWER: He didn't know anything about women at all.

DIDION: No, nothing. And the writing was so clotted and sentimental. It didn't work for me on any level.

INTERVIEWER: Was he writing too quickly, do you think?

DIDION: I don't know, I think he just had a clotted and sentimental mind.

INTERVIEWER: You mentioned reading *Moby-Dick*. Do you do much rereading?

DIDION: I often reread *Victory*, which is maybe my favorite book in the world.

INTERVIEWER: Conrad? Really? Why?

DIDION: The story is told thirdhand. It's not a story the narrator even heard from someone who experienced it. The narrator seems to have heard it from people he runs into around the Malacca Strait. So there's this fantastic distancing of the narrative, except that when you're in the middle of it, it remains very immediate. It's incredibly skillful. I have never started a novel—I mean except the first, when I was starting a novel just to start a novel—I've never written one without rereading *Victory*. It opens up the possibilities of a novel. It makes it seem worth doing. In the same way, John and I always prepared for writing a movie by watching *The Third Man*. It's perfectly told.

INTERVIEWER: Conrad was also a huge inspiration for Naipaul, whose work you admire. What drew you to Naipaul?

DIDION: I read the nonfiction first. But the novel that really attracted me—and I still read the beginning of it now and then—is *Guerillas*. It has that bauxite factory in the opening pages, which just gives you the whole feel of that part of the world. That was a thrilling book to me. The nonfiction had the same effect on me as reading Elizabeth Hardwick—you get the sense that it's possible simply to go through life noticing things and writing them down and that this is OK, it's worth doing. That the seemingly insignificant things that most of us spend our days noticing are really significant, have meaning, and tell us something. Naipaul is a great person to read before you have to do a piece. And Edmund Wilson, his essays for *The American Earthquake*. They have that everyday-traveler-in-the-world aspect, which is the opposite of an authoritative tone.

INTERVIEWER: Was it as a student at Berkeley that you began to feel that you were a writer?

DIDION: No, it began to feel almost impossible at Berkeley because we were constantly being impressed with the fact that everybody else had done it already and better. It was very daunting to me. I didn't think I could write. It took me a couple of years after I got out of Berkeley before I dared to start writing. That academic mind-set—which was kind of shallow in my case anyway—had begun to fade. Then I did write a novel over a long period of time, *Run River*. And after that it seemed feasible that maybe I could write another one.

INTERVIEWER: You had come to New York by then and were working at *Vogue*, while writing at night. Did you see writing that novel as a way of being back in California?

DIDION: Yes, it was a way of not being homesick. But I had a really hard time getting the next book going. I couldn't get past a few notes. It was *Play It As It Lays*, but it wasn't called that—I mean it didn't have a name and it wasn't what it is. For one, it was set in New York. Then, in June of 1964, John and I went to California and I started doing pieces for *The Saturday Evening Post*. We needed the money because neither one of us was working. And during the course of doing these pieces I was out in the world enough that an actual story for this so-called second novel presented itself, and then I started writing it.

INTERVIEWER: What had you been missing about California? What were you not getting in New York?

DIDION: Rivers. I was living on the East Side, and on the weekend I'd walk over to the Hudson and then I'd walk back to the East River. I kept thinking, "All right, they are rivers, but they aren't California rivers." I really missed California rivers. Also the sun going down in the West. That's one of the big advantages to Columbia-Presbyterian hospital—you can see the sunset. There's always something missing about late afternoon to me on the East Coast. Late afternoon on the West Coast ends with the sky doing all its brilliant stuff. Here it just gets dark.

The other thing I missed was horizons. I missed that on the West Coast, too, if we weren't living at the beach, but I noticed at some point that practically every painting or lithograph I bought had a horizon in it. Because it's very soothing.

INTERVIEWER: Why did you decide to come back east in 1988?

DIDION: Part of it was that Quintana was in college here, at Barnard, and part of it was that John was between books and having a hard time getting started on a new one. He felt that it was making him stale to be in one place for a long time. We had been living in Brentwood for ten years, which was longer than we had ever lived in any one place. And I think he just thought it was time to move. I didn't particularly, but we left. Even before moving, we had a little apartment in New York. To justify having it, John felt that we had to spend some periods of time there, which was extremely inconvenient for me. The apartment in New York was not very comfortable, and on arrival you would always have to arrange to get the windows washed and get food in... It was cheaper when we stayed at the Carlyle.

INTERVIEWER: But when you finally moved to New York, was it a bad move?

DIDION: No, it was fine. It just took me about a year, maybe two years all told. The time spent looking for an apartment, selling the house in California, the actual move, having work done, remembering where I put things when I unpacked—it probably took two years out of my effective working life. Though I feel that it's been the right place to be after John died. I would not have wanted to be in a house in Brentwood Park after he died.

INTERVIEWER: Why not?

DIDION: For entirely logistical reasons. In New York I didn't need to drive to dinner. There wasn't likely to be a brush fire. I wasn't going to see a snake in the pool.

INTERVIEWER: You said that you started writing for *The Saturday Evening Post* because you and John were broke. Is that where the idea of working for movies came from—the need for cash?

DIDION: Yes it was. One of the things that had made us go to Los Angeles was we had a nutty idea that we could write for television. We had a bunch of meetings with television executives, and they would explain to us, for example, the principle of *Bonanza*. The principle of *Bonanza* was: break a leg at the Ponderosa. I looked blankly at the executive and he said, "Somebody rides into town, and to make the story work, he's got to break a leg so he's around for two weeks." So we never wrote for *Bonanza*. We did, however, have one story idea picked up by *Chrysler Theatre*. We were paid a thousand dollars for it.

That was also why we started to write for the movies. We thought of it as a way to buy time. But nobody was asking us to write movies. John and his brother Nick and I took an option on *The Panic in Needle Park* and put it together ourselves. I had read the book by James Mills and it just immediately said *movie* to me. I think that the three of us each put in a thousand dollars, which was enormous at the time.

INTERVIEWER: How did you make it work as a collaboration? What were the mechanics?

DIDION: On that one, my memory is that I wrote the treatment, which was just voices. Though whenever I say I did something, or vice versa, the other person would go over it, run it through the typewriter. It was always a back-and-forth thing.

INTERVIEWER: Did you learn anything about writing from the movie work?

DIDION: Yes. I learned a lot of fictional technique. Before I'd written movies, I never could do big set-piece scenes with a lot of different speakers—when you've got twelve people around a dinner table talking at cross purposes. I had always been impressed by other people's ability to do that. Anthony Powell comes to mind. I think the first book I did those big scenes in was *A Book of Common Prayer.*

INTERVIEWER: But screenwriting is very different from prose narrative.
DIDION: It's *not* writing. You're making notes for the director—for the director more than the actors. Sidney Pollack once told us that every screenwriter should go to the Actor's Studio because there was no better way to learn what an actor needed. I'm guilty of not thinking enough about what actors need. I think instead about what the director needs.

INTERVIEWER: John wrote that Robert De Niro asked you to write a scene in *True Confessions* without a single word of dialogue—the opposite of your treatment for *The Panic in Needle Park.*
DIDION: Yeah, which is great. It's something that every writer understands, but if you turn in a scene like that to a producer, he's going to want to know where the words are.

INTERVIEWER: At the other end of the writing spectrum, there's *The New York Review of Books* and your editor there, Robert Silvers. In the seventies you wrote for him about Hollywood, Woody Allen, Naipaul, and Patty Hearst. All of those essays were, broadly speaking, book reviews. How did you make the shift to pure reporting for the *Review?*
DIDION: In 1982, John and I were going to San Salvador, and Bob expressed interest in having one or both of us write something about it. After we'd been there a few days, it became clear that I was going to do it rather than John, because John was working on a novel. Then when I started writing it, it got very long. I gave it to Bob, in its full length, and my idea was that he would figure out something to take from it. I didn't hear from him for a long time. So I wasn't expecting much, but then he called and said he was going to run the whole thing, in three parts.

INTERVIEWER: So he was able to find the through-line of the piece?
DIDION: The through-line in "Salvador" was always pretty clear: I went somewhere, this is what I saw. Very simple, like a travel piece. How Bob edited "Salvador" was by constantly nudging me toward updates on the situation and by pointing out weaker material. When I gave him the text, for example, it had a very weak ending, which was about meeting an American

evangelical student on the flight home. In other words it was the travel piece carried to its logical and not very interesting conclusion. The way Bob led me away from this was to suggest not that I cut it (it's still there), but that I follow it—and so ground it—with a return to the political situation.

INTERVIEWER: How did you decide to write about Miami in 1987?
DIDION: Ever since the Kennedy assassination, I had wanted to do something that took place in that part of the world. I thought it was really interesting that so much of the news in America, especially if you read through the assassination hearings, was coming out of our political relations with the Caribbean and Central and South America. So when we got the little apartment in New York, I thought, Well that's something useful I can do out of New York: I can fly to Miami.

INTERVIEWER: Had you spent time down south before that?
DIDION: Yes, in 1970. I had been writing a column for *Life*, but neither *Life* nor I was happy with it. We weren't on the same page. I had a contract, so if I turned something in, they had to pay me. But it was soul-searing to turn things in that didn't run. So after about seven columns, I quit. It was agreed that I would do longer pieces. And I said that I was interested in driving around the Gulf Coast, and somehow that got translated into "The Mind of the White South." I had a theory that if I could understand the South, I would understand something about California, because a lot of the California settlers came from the Border South. So I wanted to look into that. It turned out that what I was actually interested in was the South as a gateway to the Caribbean. I should have known that at the time because my original plan had been to drive all over the Gulf Coast.

We began that trip in New Orleans and spent a week there. New Orleans was fantastic. Then we drove around the Mississippi Coast, and that was fantastic too, but in New Orleans, you get a strong sense of the Caribbean. I used a lot of that week in New Orleans in *Common Prayer*. It was the most interesting place I had been in a long time. It was a week in which everything everybody said was astonishing to me.

INTERVIEWER: Three years later you started writing for *The New York Review of Books*. Was that daunting? In your essay "Why I Write" you express trepidation about intellectual, or ostensibly intellectual, matters. What freed you up enough to do that work for Bob?

DIDION: His trust. Nothing else. I couldn't even have imagined it if he hadn't responded. He recognized that it was a learning experience for me. Domestic politics, for example, was something I simply knew nothing about. And I had no interest. But Bob kept pushing me in that direction. He is really good at ascertaining what might interest you at any given moment and then just throwing a bunch of stuff at you that might or might not be related, and letting you go with it.

When I went to the political conventions in 1988—it was the first time I'd ever been to a convention—he would fax down to the hotel the front pages of *The New York Times* and *The Washington Post*. Well, you know, if there's anything you can get at a convention it's a newspaper. But he just wanted to make sure.

And then he's meticulous once you turn in a piece, in terms of making you plug in all relevant information so that everything gets covered and defended before the letters come. He spent a lot of time, for example, making sure that I acknowledged all the issues in the Terri Schiavo piece, which had the potential for eliciting strong reactions. He's the person I trust more than anybody.

INTERVIEWER: Why do you think he pushed you to write about politics?
DIDION: I think he had a sense that I would be outside it enough.

INTERVIEWER: No insider reporting—you didn't know anyone.
DIDION: I didn't even know their names!

INTERVIEWER: But now your political writing has a very strong point of view—you take sides. Is that something that usually happens during the reporting process, or during the writing?
DIDION: If I am sufficiently interested in a political situation to write a piece about it, I generally have a point of view, although I don't usually recognize it. Something about a situation will bother me, so I will write a piece to find out what it is that bothers me.

INTERVIEWER: When you moved into writing about politics, you moved away from the more personal writing you'd been doing. Was that a deliberate departure?
DIDION: Yes, I was bored. For one thing, that kind of writing is limiting. Another reason was that I was getting a very strong response from readers,

which was depressing because there was no way for me to reach out and help them back. I didn't want to become Miss Lonelyhearts.

INTERVIEWER: And the pieces on El Salvador were the first in which politics really drive the narrative.

DIDION: Actually it was a novel, *Common Prayer*. We had gone to a film festival in Cartagena and I got sick there, some kind of salmonella. We left Cartagena and went to Bogotá, and then we came back to Los Angeles and I was sick for about four months. I started doing a lot of reading about South America, where I'd never been. There's a passage by Christopher Isherwood in a book of his called *The Condor and the Cows*, in which he describes arriving in Venezuela and being astonished to think that it had been down there every day of his life. That was the way that I felt about South America. Then later I started reading a lot about Central America because it was becoming clear to me that my novel had to take place in a rather small country. So that was when I started thinking more politically.

INTERVIEWER: But it still didn't push you into an interest in domestic politics.

DIDION: I didn't get the connection. I don't know why I didn't get the connection, since I wasn't interested in the politics of these countries per se, but rather in how American foreign policy affected them. And the extent to which we are involved abroad is entirely driven by our own domestic politics. So I don't know why I didn't get that.

I started to get this in *Salvador*, but not fully until *Miami*. Our policy with Cuba and with exiles has been totally driven by domestic politics. It still is. But it was very hard for me to understand the process of domestic politics. I could get the overall picture, but the actual words people said were almost unintelligible to me.

INTERVIEWER: How did it become clearer?

DIDION: I realized that the words didn't have any actual meaning, that they described a negotiation more than they described an idea. But then you begin to see that the lack of specificity is specific in itself, that it is an obscuring device.

INTERVIEWER: Did it help you when you were working on *Salvador* and *Miami* to talk to the political figures you were writing about?

DIDION: In those cases it did. Though, I didn't talk to a lot of American politicians. I remember talking to the then-president of El Salvador, who was astounding. We were talking about a new land reform law and I explained that I couldn't quite understand what was being said about it. We were discussing a provision—Provision 207—that seemed to me to say that landowners could arrange their affairs so as to be unaffected by the reform.

He said, 207 always applied only to 1979. That is what no one understands. I asked, "Did he mean that 207 applied only to 1979 because no landowner would work against his interests by allowing tenants on his land after 207 took effect?" He said, "Exactly, no one would rent out land under 207. They would have to be crazy to do that."

Well, that was forthright. There are very few politicians who would say exactly.

INTERVIEWER: Was it helpful to talk with John about your experiences there?

DIDION: It was useful to talk to him about politics because he viscerally understood politics. He grew up in an Irish Catholic family in Hartford, a town where politics was part of what you ate for breakfast. I mean, it didn't take *him* a long time to understand that nobody was saying anything.

INTERVIEWER: After *Salvador*, you wrote your next novel, *Democracy*. It seems informed by the reporting you were doing about America's relationship to the world.

DIDION: The fall of Saigon, though it takes place offstage, was the main thing on my mind. Saigon fell while I was teaching at Berkeley in 1975. I couldn't get those images out of my head, and that was the strongest impulse behind *Democracy*. When the book came out, some people wondered why it began with the bomb tests in the Pacific, but I think those bomb tests formed a straight line to pushing the helicopters off the aircraft carriers when we were abandoning Saigon. It was a very clear progression in my mind. Mainly, I wanted to show that you could write a romance and still have the fall of Saigon, or the Iran-Contra affair. It would be hard for me to stay with a novel if I didn't see a very strong personal story at the center of it.

Democracy is really a much more complete version of *Common Prayer*, with basically the same structure. There is a narrator who tries to understand the character who's being talked about and reconstruct the story. I had a very clear picture in my mind of both those women, but I couldn't tell the story without standing way far away. Charlotte, in *Common Prayer*, was somebody who had a very expensive dress with a seam that was coming out. There was a kind of fevered carelessness to her. *Democracy* started out as a comedy, a comic novel. And I think that there is a more even view of life in it. I had a terrible time with it. I don't know why, but it never got easy.

In Brentwood, we had a big safe-deposit box to put manuscripts in if we left town during fire season. It was such a big box that we never bothered to clean it out. When we were moving, in 1988, and I had to go through the box, I found I don't know how many different versions of the first ninety pages of *Democracy*, with different dates on them, written over several years. I would write ninety pages and not be able to go any further. I couldn't make the switch. I don't know how that was solved. Many of those drafts began with Billy Dillon coming to Amagansett to tell Inez that her father had shot her sister. It was very hard to get from there to any place. It didn't work. It was too conventional a narrative. I never hit the spot where I could sail through. I never got to that point, even at the very end.

INTERVIEWER: Was that a first for you?

DIDION: It was a first for a novel. I really did not think I was going to finish it two nights before I finished it. And when I did finish it, I had a sense that I was just abandoning it, that I was just calling it. It was sort of like Vietnam itself—why don't we just say we've won and leave? I didn't have a real sense of completion about it.

INTERVIEWER: Your novels are greatly informed by the travel and reporting you do for your nonfiction. Do you ever do research specifically for the fiction?

DIDION: *Common Prayer* was researched. We had someone working for us, Tina Moore, who was a fantastic researcher. She would go to the UCLA library, and I would say, "Bring me back anything on plantation life in Central America." And she would come back and say, "This is really what you're looking for—you'll love this." And it would not be plantation life in Central America. It would be Ceylon, but it would be fantastic. She had an instinct for what was the same story, and what I was looking for. What I was looking for were rules for living in the tropics. I didn't know that, but that's what I found. In *Democracy* I was more familiar with all the places.

INTERVIEWER: The last novel you wrote was *The Last Thing He Wanted*. That came out in 1996. Had you been working on it for a long time?

DIDION: No. I started it in the early fall or late summer of 1995, and I finished it at Christmas. It was a novel I had been thinking about writing for a while. I wanted to write a novel about the Iran-Contra affair, and get in all that stuff that was being lost. Basically it's a novel about Miami. I wanted it to be very densely plotted. I noticed that conspiracy was central to understanding that part of the world; everybody was always being set up in some way. The plot was going to be so complicated that I was going to have to write it fast or I wouldn't be able to keep it all in my head. If I forgot one little detail it wouldn't work, and half the readers didn't understand what happened in the end. Many people thought that Elena tried to kill Treat Morrison. Why did she want to kill him? They would ask me. But she didn't. Someone else did, and set her up. Apparently I didn't make that clear.

I had begun to lose patience with the conventions of writing. Descriptions went first; in both fiction and nonfiction, I just got impatient with those long paragraphs of description. By which I do not mean—obviously—the single detail that gives you the scene. I'm talking about description as a substitute for thinking. I think you can see me losing my patience as early as *Democracy*. That was why that book was so hard to write.

INTERVIEWER: After *Democracy* and *Miami*, and before *The Last Thing He Wanted*, there was the nonfiction collection *After Henry*, which strikes me as a way of coming back to New York and trying to understand what the city was.

DIDION: It has that long piece "Sentimental Journeys," about the Central Park jogger, which began with that impulse. We had been in New York a year or two, and I realized that I was living here without engaging the city at all. I might as well have been living in another city, because I didn't understand it, I didn't get it. So I realized that I needed to do some reporting on it. Bob and I decided I would do a series of short reporting pieces on New York, and the first one would be about the jogger. But it wasn't really reporting. It was coming at a situation from a lot of angles. I got so involved in it that, by the time I finished the piece, it was too long. I turned it in and Bob had some comments—many, many comments, which caused it to be even longer because he thought it needed so much additional material, which he was right about. By the time I'd plugged it all in, I'd added another six to eight thousand words. When I finally had finished it, I thought, That's all I have to do about New York.

INTERVIEWER: Although it is about the city, "Sentimental Journeys" is really about race and class and money.

DIDION: It seemed to me that the case was treated with a lot of contempt by the people who were handling it.

INTERVIEWER: How so?

DIDION: The prosecution thought they had the press and popular sentiment on their side. The case became a way of expressing the city's rage at being broke and being in another recession and not having a general comfort level, the sense that there were people sleeping on the streets—which there were. We moved here six months after the '87 stock market crash. Over the next couple of years, its effect on Madison Avenue was staggering. You could not walk down Madison Avenue at eight in the evening without having to avoid stepping on people sleeping in every doorway. There was a German television crew here doing a piece on the jogger, and they wanted to shoot in Harlem, but it was late in the day and they were losing the light. They kept asking me what the closest place was where they could shoot and see poverty. I said, "Try Seventy-second and Madison." You know where Polo is now? That building was empty and the padlocks were broken and you could see rats scuttling around inside. The landlord had emptied it—I presume because he wanted to get higher rents—and then everything had crashed. There was nothing there. That entire block was a mess.

INTERVIEWER: So from California you had turned your attention to the third world, and now you were able to recognize New York because of the work you had done in the third world.

DIDION: A lot of what I had seen as New York's sentimentality is derived from the stories the city tells itself to rationalize its class contradictions. I didn't realize that until I started doing the jogger piece. Everything started falling into place on that piece. Bob would send me clips about the trial, but on this one I was on my own, because only I knew where it was going.

INTERVIEWER: In some of your early essays on California, your subject matter was as distinctively your own as your writing style. In recent decades, though, it's not so much the story but your take on the story that makes your work distinctive.

DIDION: The shift came about as I became more confident that my own take was worth doing. In the beginning, I didn't want to do any stories that anyone else was doing. As time went by, I got more comfortable with that. For example, on the Central Park jogger piece I could not get into the courtroom because I didn't have a police pass. This forced me into another approach, which turned out to be a more interesting one. At least to me.

INTERVIEWER: Wasn't it around the same time that you were also doing the "Letter from Los Angeles" for Robert Gottlieb at *The New Yorker*?

DIDION: Yes. Though I wasn't doing more than two of those a year. I think they only ran six to eight thousand words, but the idea was to do several things in each letter. I had never done that before, where you just really discuss what people are talking about that week. It was easy to do. It was a totally different tone from the *Review*. I went over those *New Yorker* pieces when I collected them. I probably took out some of the *New Yorker*'s editing, which is just their way of making everything sound a certain way.

INTERVIEWER: Can you characterize your methods as a reporter?

DIDION: I can't ask anything. Once in a while if I'm forced into it I will conduct an interview, but it's usually pro forma, just to establish my credentials as somebody who's allowed to hang around for a while. It doesn't matter to me what people say to me in the interview because I don't trust it. Sometimes you do interviews where you get a lot. But you don't get them from public figures.

When I was conducting interviews for the piece on Lakewood, it was essential to do interviews because that was the whole point. But these were not public figures. On the one hand, we were discussing what I was ostensibly there doing a piece about, which was the Spur Posse, a group of local high school boys who had been arrested for various infractions. But on the other hand, we were talking, because it was the first thing on everyone's mind, about the defense industry going downhill, which was what the town was about. That was a case in which I did interviewing and listened.

INTERVIEWER: Did the book about California, *Where I Was From*, grow out of that piece, or had you already been thinking about a book?

DIDION: I had actually started a book about California in the seventies. I had written some of that first part, which is about my family, but I could never go anywhere with it for two reasons. One was that I still hadn't figured out California. The other was that I didn't want to figure out California because whatever I figured out would be different from the California my mother and father had told me about. I didn't want to engage that.

INTERVIEWER: You felt like you were still their child?

DIDION: I just didn't see any point in engaging it. By the time I did the book, they were dead.

INTERVIEWER: You said earlier that after *The White Album* you were tired of personal writing and didn't want to become Miss Lonelyhearts. You must be getting a larger personal response from readers than ever with *The Year of Magical Thinking*. Is that difficult?

DIDION: I have been getting a very strong emotional response to *Magical Thinking*. But it's not a crazy response; it's not demanding. It's people trying to make sense of a fairly universal experience that most people don't talk about. So this is a case in which I have found myself able to deal with the response directly.

INTERVIEWER: Do you ever think you might go back to the idea of doing little pieces about New York?

DIDION: I don't know. It is still a possibility, but my basic question about New York was answered for me: it's criminal.

INTERVIEWER: That was your question?

DIDION: Yes, it's criminal.

INTERVIEWER: Do you find it stimulating in some way to live here?

DIDION: I find it really comfortable. During the time we lived in California, which lasted twenty-four years, I didn't miss New York after the first year. And after the second year I started to think of New York as sentimental. There were periods when I didn't even come to New York at all. One time I realized that I had been to Hong Kong twice since I had last been to New York. Then we started spending more time in New York. Both John and I were really happy to have been here on 9/11. I can't think of any place else I would have rather been on 9/11, and in the immediate aftermath.

INTERVIEWER: You could have stayed in Sacramento forever as a novelist, but you started to move out into the worlds of Hollywood and politics.

DIDION: I was never a big fan of people who don't leave home. I don't know why. It just seems part of your duty in life.

INTERVIEWER: I'm reminded of Charlotte in *A Book of Common Prayer*. She has no conception of the outside world but she wants to be in it.

DIDION: Although a novel takes place in the larger world, there's always some drive in it that is entirely personal—even if you don't know it while you're doing it. I realized some years after *A Book of Common Prayer* was finished that it was about my anticipating Quintana's growing up. I wrote it around 1975, so she would have been nine, but I was already anticipating separation and actually working through that ahead of time. So novels are also about things you're afraid you can't deal with.

INTERVIEWER: Are you working on one now?
DIDION: No. I haven't felt that I wanted to bury myself for that intense a period.

INTERVIEWER: You want to be in the world a bit.
DIDION: Yeah. A little bit.

Seeing Things Straight

Gibson Fay-Leblanc / 2006

From *Guernica,* April 15, 2006. © 2006 by Gibson Fay-Leblanc. Reprinted by permission.

Acclaim for Joan Didion's *The Year of Magical Thinking* has been near-universal. Lauded in newspapers and magazines throughout the country, it was awarded the 2005 National Book Award and hailed as a "masterpiece of two genres: memoir and investigative journalism." Author of five novels, eight books of nonfiction, and many screenplays, Didion is perhaps best known for her essays. Whether she's writing on the Central Park jogger case, the Hoover Dam, John Wayne, the Haight-Ashbury district of San Francisco in the late sixties, El Salvador in the early eighties, or post 9/11 politics, Didion insists on the complexities of actual life rather than a more simplified narrative. On many occasions she has seemed all too eager to turn that examination onto herself as well.

One of her best-known essays, "The White Album," considers the chaos of the late sixties and early seventies and begins, "We tell ourselves stories in order to live." Didion then makes us see how she has begun to doubt all of her own stories. Juxtaposed in the first few pages of that essay are the author's citation as *Los Angeles Times* "Woman of the Year" and an excerpt from her psychiatrist's report describing her frayed mental state.

If you have heard of her latest book, thanks to its wide acclaim, you have no doubt heard the story that underlies it: while Didion and her husband of nearly forty years, the writer John Gregory Dunne, were dealing with their daughter's life-threatening illness, one night at the dinner table after returning home from the ICU, Dunne had a heart attack and died. Didion's daughter, Quintana, later recovered and attended her father's funeral, only to suffer a massive hematoma two months later and die at the age of thirty-nine. Searching through everything from T. S. Eliot to Emily Post's *Etiquette*, and Euripides to clinical neuroscience, Didion's book tries to get at the roots

126

of grief and to consider why hers led to the hope that her husband would return, despite a long history of critiquing the "sentimental narratives" of our individual and collective thinking.

Didion is currently working on a one-woman play based on her experiences, to be directed by David Hare. Her collected nonfiction, *We Tell Ourselves Stories in Order to Live*, will be released this fall. In April, Didion can be found reading a favorite poem, Gerard Manley Hopkins' "Carrion Comfort," on www.knopfpoetry.com.

Guernica: When people describe your work, they often talk about your sentences. In general, the sentences in your nonfiction tend to be more complicated than in your fiction—more winding, more filled with "sinkholes" (as you once said about Henry James'[s] sentences). Yet your sentences in *The Year of Magical Thinking* seem to be simpler, or of a different order.

Joan Didion: I was trying to write without style. I didn't want to falsify in any way by letting the style carry [the book]. I wanted it raw as opposed to polished—usually, I want polish—but this I wanted raw. I thought it was raw until I saw an edit of it with copyediting. Then it became clear to me that it was written as opposed to not written. I had thought I was not writing it.

Guernica: When you say you wanted it raw, did that mean worrying over the sentences less, trying to write faster?

Joan Didion: Worrying over them less, yes. And not fretting transitions. I was relying on a kind of natural transition—the transitions made by someone who is slightly deranged.

Guernica: You once said that the discovery in nonfiction happens in the research rather than in the writing.

Joan Didion: Actually, it doesn't. It still happens in the writing. You start [in nonfiction] with a whole lot more going for you, because all the discovery isn't waiting to be made. You've made some of it in the research. As you get deeper into a piece and do more research, the notes are in the direction of the piece—you're actually writing it.

Guernica: In comparison with your other nonfiction pieces, was there more discovery in the writing of *The Year of Magical Thinking*?

Joan Didion: The whole thing was discovery. In retrospect, it is about a search for my own sanity and the discovery that I have it.

Guernica: You did many readings and interviews for this book. Considering how an author on a book tour gets asked the same questions over and over, was that kind of repetition difficult? Was it therapeutic in some way?

Joan Didion: Doing that promotion was very therapeutic at the time I did it for two reasons. One, my daughter had just died, about two weeks before. Actually, I was in the middle of doing the New York promotion even as she died, as she was dying. [The promotion] was a way of maintaining a kind of momentum that I might not have been able to maintain otherwise.

I did not find this a hard book to talk about. If you are out promoting a book on politics, it requires a reader who knows exactly what you know to have a conversation, which isn't always what you find. And even you don't know what you know when you're in the middle of doing promotion, because you're just not focused. You're not sitting at your computer with all of the notes in front of you. You can be asked a simple question, and you tend to forget names. There was no chance of forgetting anybody's name in this book.

Guernica: What about after the book tour was over? What about the return to "normal" life?

Joan Didion: I haven't totally returned to normal life. I went into working almost directly afterwards on the play.

Guernica: Was that by design?

Joan Didion: Yes. Again, momentum.

Guernica: You write in the book about your husband's participation in your writing. In what ways have you had to relearn your writing process now that your husband and first reader is gone?

Joan Didion: The first piece that I wrote after John died—it was a long time after he died—was a piece about the campaigns in September 2004. I found that really hard to do because he had always read everything. That was hard in one way. I didn't miss him writing [*The Year of Magical Thinking*] because I had the sense—I'm not talking about any kind of mystical stuff—that he was right there with me when I was writing it. I knew what he would say because I was so focused on him while I was writing it. I didn't have any sense of missing him.

Right now, I wish I could talk to him about what to do next. He was very acute on what would be the right thing to do and what would be something that would run itself out without completion.

I also wish he was here to answer the phone [*laughs*].

Guernica: At what point in the writing of *Magical Thinking* did you decide to place repetition at the heart of the book's structure?

Joan Didion: It was before I started to write the book. I had been typing some notes about Quintana's illness—doctors and telephone numbers—when I started making some other notes about John's death. Then at some point I found myself wondering how to structure it. I realized that if I was thinking about how to structure it, I was thinking about a book. It occurred to me a day or so later that the only possible way to structure it was to replicate the experience, to repeat, to run the tape over and over and over again, looking for a different ending. I thought you would keep coming at these key [details], and each time you would see them at a slightly different angle—they would reveal themselves slightly differently.

Guernica: How did you know which particular parts of the tape or which phrases would repeat?

Joan Didion: It was intuitive. The simplest way it happens is that something comes to your mind again.

Guernica: You've said that writing is a hostile act, and you've also compared writing and acting and talked about writing as 'make-believe,' writing as 'performance.' Have you found these ways of thinking about it to be as true of this book as of your other books?

Joan Didion: This was less of a performance. That was what I was trying to stay away from. And, actually, it wasn't a hostile act. A lot of what I write is hostile, but this wasn't. This was an experience where I found myself for the first time without any control or answers, so it was just about being disoriented.

Guernica: How did the idea to adapt the book into a Broadway play come about?

Joan Didion: Scott Rudin, who's producing it, came to me and said that he thought it would make a good one-woman play, and I resisted this idea. But he kept talking about it; and, after a while, I started thinking it would be an interesting thing to do, an interesting thing to try. I've never written a play or tried to write a play. I thought it would be an interesting exercise, and it has been. I've done a couple of drafts—I'm in the middle of it now.

Guernica: Did you have any trepidation about working in a new genre?

Joan Didion: That was what was attractive about it. My trepidation was in staying with the material, but it actually isn't the same material, as it's turned out, as time has passed. And also, it's a new form, so it feels different to me.

Guernica: How does one go about adapting a memoir like this, so much of which involves your own explorations of grief, into a play?

Joan Didion: That's what the play is about too. It's just one woman on a stage, so the challenge there is to make you want to continue looking at that woman on the stage.

Guernica: You've done quite a bit of screenwriting, mostly with your husband. Are there things that are transferable between screenwriting and playwriting?

Joan Didion: No, none. Once in a while there were things in screenwriting that taught me things for fiction. But there's nothing in screenwriting that teaches you anything for the theater. I'm not sure I've ever fully appreciated before how different a form theater is.

Guernica: How would you distinguish screenwriting from playwriting or playwriting from fiction?

Joan Didion: Something I've always known and said and thought about the screen is that if it's anything in the world, it's literal. It's so literal that there's a whole lot you can't do because you're stuck with the literalness of the screen. The stage is not literal.

Guernica: What about thinking about how a piece of fiction works versus how a play works?

Joan Didion: They're more alike than not. It's a question of finding a structure and a rhythm, and withholding and giving, and knowing when to do those things.

Guernica: Can we expect you to do more political writing?

Joan Didion: I want to go back to it. It's bracing, it's another form of momentum.

Guernica: You've written many essays about "the process"—the false narratives of politics as compared with the actual life of the country. Are there any politicians out there currently who cut through these false narratives or who are closer to the actual life of the country?

Joan Didion: I don't know these politicians. Chuck Hagel is generally seen as someone who's unelectable because he doesn't follow a false narrative. And McCain used to be seen that way too, although [these days] he's doing a pretty good job of following a narrative. Obviously, there have been people in American political life who have been closer to the life of the country—I think Jerry Brown was closer to the life of the country.

Guernica: Do you see any signs that we're starting to come out of the post-9/11 sentimental narrative, the era of "fixed opinions" and lack of discussion that you wrote about in the *New York Review of Books* in 2003?
Joan Didion: No, I think we're still in it. Maybe it's because everyone got so bludgeoned by those fixed opinions, but no one even seems to notice the contradictions anymore. I don't mean nobody notices, but, well, I'm an idealist I suppose, because I always think large numbers of Americans are going to rise up.

Guernica: There is certainly more discussion and dissent in terms of Iraq.
Joan Didion: There certainly is, but we'll have to wait and see what it adds up to, if it's going to make any difference.

Guernica: In so much of your nonfiction, your authority as a writer and observer is at issue. You go to great lengths to establish it and undermine it, sometimes at the same time. Did you feel a different kind of authority in writing this most recent book because it's so steeped in your experiences of loss?
Joan Didion: The narrative, if there is one, is of someone trying to see if she's sane or insane. A lot of what I was thinking during the year would make me think I'm insane. So, yeah, I think I was still undermining the narrative there.

Guernica: So much of your writing is concerned with the sentimental narratives we have, these myths that keep us going that are only loosely, if at all, tied to our actual lives or to reality. I suppose the "magical thinking" that you describe is a kind of subconscious narrative-making, and it also seems like a self-protective mechanism that helped you not face your husband's death fully right away. I'm wondering if you think this kind of "magical thinking" was necessary or important.
Joan Didion: There's a conflict in my mind about that. I think it was useful, it had a role in keeping me together. But, at the same time, I have an investment in not being crazy. I have a real investment in seeing things straight. This runs counter to that investment, so it required giving up an idea of myself, the idea being that I had control.

Guernica: Having written the book and talked about it at length, have you found yourself still thinking this way?

Joan Didion: To some extent, yes. But I'm so practiced in evading it now, in hiding it. I still haven't cleaned out John's closets, but I don't have time to [*laughs*].

Joan Didion Remembers
The Panic in Needle Park

Aaron Hillis / 2009

From ifc.com, January 28, 2009. © 2009 by Aaron Hillis. Reprinted by permission.

Journalist, novelist, essayist and all-around elegant wordsmith Joan Didion won the National Book Award in 2005 for *The Year of Magical Thinking*, a memoir and instant classic about the year following the death of her husband John Gregory Dunne. With her late partner, Didion co-wrote such screenplays as *True Confessions*, *Up Close [and] Personal* and *A Star is Born* (the Babs version, naturally), as well as the best of the lot, an adaptation of James Mills'[s] novel *The Panic in Needle Park*. Released in 1971, director Jerry Schatzberg's stark, moving, gorgeously photographed drama refers to the triangular Manhattan intersection at Broadway and 72nd Street—now dubbed Sherman Square, but then a hotbed for heroin junkies. A brilliant but at the time unknown Al Pacino stars as a small-time pusher who falls for smacked-out Midwesterner Kitty Winn (who won the Best Actress award at Cannes for her role), their story not so much a rise-and-fall chronicle as much as a fallen-and-fallen-further saga of love and betrayal. Ten minutes is never enough time with an interviewee as erudite as Didion, but the literary icon was kind enough to chat this past weekend in honor of the *Panic* re-release at New York City's Film Forum.

Aaron Hillis: When you read *The Panic in Needle Park* in the summer of 1967, what was it that appealed to you for a potential screenplay adaptation?
Joan Didion: The love story. Plain and simple, that was it. It was an interesting world that we hadn't seen on the screen in exactly that way, so I just felt as if it could work. As written by James Mills, it had a good strong narrative, you know?

Hillis: At the time, what did or didn't you know about the life of heroin junkies on Manhattan's West Side?

Didion: I was living in California at the time. I knew a little more about other drugs because I had just [written] a long piece on the Haight-Ashbury, but heroin was not one of the drugs that was in play. What did I know about it? I didn't know really about that life, so we did some research. We stayed at the Alamac Hotel [at Broadway and West 71st] for two or three weeks.

Hillis: Besides your experience co-writing it, does the film itself mean anything differently to you now?

Didion: I saw part of it on television one night about a year ago. Before that, I hadn't seen it in a long time. There wasn't a DVD of it until last year. I'd like to think it held up [*laughs*]. I kind of have to think that. When a picture is shooting, a lot of things seem arbitrary, or you might've done them differently if you thought twice about it. When we were shooting, I was overcome with what I had failed to do. Actually, when I saw it [again], I was struck by how much we *did* do. I can't reconstruct exactly what. When you're making a picture, you're hypersensitive to everything that might be wrong with it or might not work. You don't see what's right quite often. It can work the other way, too, but this is one that happily worked the good way [*laughs*]. It's fascinating to me that there's still an air of romanticism about New York of that era, as if it was more alive and creative when it was riddled with crime, drugs, and sleaze.

That was a nasty part of town. I was amazed to drive back by there and see apartments on that very corner being advertised on the side of a building, starting at $1.5 million. I'm happier with the cleaned up [New York of today]. You can still find un-cleaned-up parts [*laughs*]. Just not at the corner of 72nd and Broadway.

Hillis: In your 1973 essay "In Hollywood," you were rather caustic towards film criticism. Do you still feel it's a "peculiarly vaporous" occupation?

Didion: I think the phrase I used was "petit-point-on-Kleenex," and a lot of it seemed to have that situation. But no, I think people know more about film now than they knew then. And I think critics really have a more accurate sense of how pictures are put together, and why certain things work the way they do. People know a little more about the business. There were so many great pictures in the seventies; I think, gradually, people were looking at them in a serious way.

Joan Didion: Crafting an Elegy for Her Daughter

Terry Gross / 2011

From *Fresh Air,* broadcast November 2, 2011. © 2011 by NPR. *Fresh Air with Terry Goss* is produced by WHYY, Inc. in Philadelphia and distributed by NPR. Podcasts are available at ww.npr.org/podcasts and on iTunes. Reprinted by permission.

Joan Didion has spent the past few years reporting on her grief. Her best-selling memoir *The Year of Magical Thinking* was about the year following the death of her husband, the writer John Gregory Dunne. He died at the very end of 2003 of a heart attack at the age of seventy-one. At that time, their daughter, Quintana Roo, was in the hospital in a coma suffering from pneumonia and septic shock. In August 2005, just a few weeks before the publication of *The Year of Magical Thinking,* Didion's daughter died of pancreatitis after spending much of the previous two years in ICUs. Now Joan Didion has written a memoir reflecting on her daughter's life and death and on what she fears were her own shortcomings as a mother. It's called *Blue Nights* and it's about a period when Didion says she found her "mind turning increasingly to illness, to the end of promise, the dwindling of the days, the inevitability of the fading, the dying of the brightness."

Terry Gross: I get the feeling you wrote this book because you couldn't write anything else, because all you could think about was the death of your daughter.

Joan Didion: That's right. I didn't actually want to write it. I had some dim idea that it was a much less personal book than it turned out to be.

TG: Combined with the grief that you have for your daughter, you're also feeling the frailty that comes with aging, and you have a lot of nerve pain that you've been experiencing. So you've had like the total package, physical and emotional pain at the same time. Do you tend to be obsessive about physical pain or emotional pain?

JD: Well, I try not to be. Let us put it that way (*laughter*). But it doesn't always work out.

TG: If you're trying to examine that pain, whether it's your physical pain or your grief, and report on it in a book, does it put some distance between you and the grief or you and the pain because you're standing back and examining it and describing it?

JD: I have always found that if I examine something it's less scary. You know, I grew up in the West and we always had this theory that if you kept the snake in your eyeline the snake wasn't going to bite you. And that's kind of the way I feel about confronting pain. I want to know where it is.

TG: Your daughter, Quintana, died in 2005, six weeks before the publication of your memoir about losing your husband. When the book about your husband was published and I interviewed you, you said that you hadn't yet started mourning for your daughter.

JD: I don't think I started mourning for her until I started writing this book.

TG: Could you only do one at a time?

JD: Definitely, I could only do one at a time. And I couldn't in any way confront the death of my daughter for a long time.

TG: Why?

JD: Because she was adopted. She had been given to me to take care of and I had failed to do that. There was a huge guilt at work.

TG: What do you mean you failed to do that? A parent can't protect a child from death.

JD: But don't we all try. We try to keep our children safe. That's pretty much what parents are put on this earth to do.

TG: Now you've said that when you lost your husband it was like losing part of yourself. He could complete your sentences, he could be your protection from the world. But when your daughter died it raised so many questions for you about responsibility and guilt. *Were you a good mother? Did you adequately protect her?* One of the things I think you fear you were at fault for was not picking up on how troubled she was.

JD: Of course. She was much more troubled than I ever recognized or admitted. Because at the same time she was very troubled, she was infinitely amusing and charming. And that's naturally what I tended to focus on. I say *naturally* because I think most of us go through life trying to focus on what works for us, and her amusing side definitely worked for me.

TG: But she had been diagnosed with depression, obsessive-compulsive disorder, borderline personality disorder . . .
JD: The whole gamut.

TG: And looking back you think you maybe could have seen that earlier.
JD: I certainly could have seen it earlier. I don't know what I would have done about it. What we can see and what we can do about what we see are two different matters for parents usually.

TG: And I think an example you give in the book is she had an assignment to write a journal—it was a school assignment—and she gave it to you to edit, and you were kind of line editing it, suggesting different words, when you realized you weren't paying attention to the pain that she was expressing in this journal.
JD: Exactly. Which is kind of the way we tend to deal with our children. Later we realize that maybe we haven't been listening to them at all. We've been listening to the very edge of what they say without letting it sink in.

TG: You adopted your daughter after trying to conceive for a couple of years. You were thirty-one when the adoption came through. But for years before that you were adamant about not getting pregnant. You so much didn't want to get pregnant. What changed your mind?
JD: It just came over me suddenly. I could almost date it if I remembered what year it was. But suddenly I had to have a baby. I started cutting out pictures of babies from magazines and sticking them on the wall in my bedroom. I have no idea why that came over me at that moment, but it became really necessary. And then, lo and behold, a baby was in my house.

TG: Yeah, you got a call from a doctor who was an obstetrician-gynecologist—
JD:—a gynecologist, yeah—

TG:—and who delivered the baby, and the mother wanted to give it up for adoption, and you became the mother. So after you got the call, the baby,

Quintana, remained in the hospital for a couple of nights, and those two nights you say you had dreams about forgetting you had a baby, leaving the baby in the drawer and then going out to dinner without making provisions to feed her.

JD: I had dreams about leaving the baby uncared for while I did something that I would have done before she was born, like decide to stay in town for a movie and dinner. All of these things that we do without thinking before we have children, and then suddenly we don't do them anymore and it comes home to us in a real way that it's very different to have the responsibility of a child.

TG: And you write, too—this is right before you take home the baby—"What if I fail to take care of this baby? What if this baby fails to thrive? What if this baby fails to love me? And worse yet . . . what if I fail to love this baby?"

JD: That's something that we don't talk about very much, but almost everybody I know who has ever had a child is afraid before the baby comes that they won't like the baby or love the baby, that they won't be up to it.

TG: So what was the reality when you brought Quintana home? Did you still fear that you wouldn't love her, did you still fear that you would leave her in the drawer?

JD: No, no, no, no, no. The reality actually couldn't have been more perfect. I remember leaving the hospital with her and driving—we were living down on the beach then—and we were on the San Diego Freeway going home and I always thought of myself as bonding with her on the San Diego.

TG: Quintana was born in 1966, and this is like the early stages of the women's movement, and I think women then were working so hard to figure out what it meant to be a mother with still having some sense of equality and without giving up your work and the life and identity that you had created outside the home. Were you trying to figure that out for yourself?

JD: Actually, no I wasn't. It never crossed my mind that I would have to figure it out. I always thought I would be working. And I always thought I would have a baby if I was lucky enough. So I wasn't as troubled by that. When I got troubled by it was when I realized I wasn't really doing it as well as I had anticipated I would be able to.

TG: You had planned a trip to Saigon for a magazine piece, and the trip was to take place shortly after you adopted Quintana. You didn't know that you were on the verge of becoming a mother when you accepted the Saigon piece?

JD: No.

TG: So you say that you had planned on going on the trip anyway, bringing Quintana with you. You brought a beautiful flowered silk parasol to protect her from the sun. And you realized you were acting as if you were going to a high-fashion place with her and that you weren't dealing with the reality here.

JD: Right. It was all going to be tea and lemon presses at *Le Cirques Beautiffe*. I wasn't seeing that there was an actual shooting war—a bad, bad war going on, this was 1966—we were kind of at the worst turn in it.

TG: In the Vietnam War?

JD: In the Vietnam War.

TG: You say you were raising Quintana like a doll. What do you mean by that?

JD: When I say I was raising her like a doll, I mean literally I was dressing her. That was my main conception of my role. I made sure that her clothes were taken care of. I dressed her. She was a doll to me, which in retrospect gave me probably a distorted idea of who she was. I didn't give her enough credit for being a grown-up person. Even as a four-year-old she was a grown-up person.

TG: When did that change for you? When did you start feeling like she wasn't a doll and there was more than dressing her?

JD: Oh, when she was twelve, thirteen, when she was beginning to be in high school. Then the reality that this was a real person started coming through to me.

TG: It's hard for me to imagine that when she was ten and eleven you were still treating her as a doll.

JD: Well, maybe less when she was ten or eleven.

TG: I mean children are so demanding. It's hard to treat a child like a doll at some point because they're asking for things, they're insisting on things, they're crying, they're laughing, they're making their presence felt. They're willful.

JD: She was actually not a willful child.

TG: Because your daughter had a cerebral brain hemorrhage toward the end of her life and she was in a medically induced coma for a while, her memory was not good, her comprehension wasn't good because of these medical problems, you were, I assume, unable to talk about the things that you might have liked to talk with her about at the end of her life?

JD: No, I was able to talk with her at the end of her life because she was very open about her fears and her condition.

TG: Would it be an intrusion to ask what kinds of things you were able to talk about and maybe resolve? Did you talk about any of the fears about how you behaved as a mother, the fears you express in the book. Did you express any of those fears to her?

JD: Once we talked about what kind of mother I had been. And she, to my surprise, said, "You were okay, but you were a little remote." Now that was a very frank thing for her to say. And I recognized myself in it. I was a little remote.

TG: You write that your daughter once expressed that fear that your husband would die and there would be no one but her to take care of you.

JD: That was a scary moment.

TG: When was that?

JD: It was actually not long before she died. It was in the last few years of her life. But I had not realized how heavily she bore the responsibility of taking care of me, which hadn't occurred to me as a necessity.

TG: You think it's because she saw you as frail.

JD: I think it was because she saw me as frail.

TG: And you see yourself as frail.

JD: Well, I certainly do now. I'm not sure I did then.

TG: When you were younger and your husband and daughter were alive, did you ever expect you'd be facing the last years of your life without them, that you'd be left on your own?

JD: No, I never did expect that. I don't know why I never expected it. I mean there was no reason to think that Quintana would be ill, but John demonstrably had things that could kill him. He had heart disease that had undergone a number of interventions, and eventually one of them wasn't going to intervene. But I didn't face this. I never had a very realistic view of everybody else's survival time.

TG: Do you worry about being alone? It sounds like you like being alone but you hate being alone.
JD: I love being alone. I need to be alone. I get terribly anxious and nervous if I'm not alone for a period of enough time.

TG: Are there objects from your husband or daughter that you actually want to look at every now and then and that bring back good memories, like helpful memories?
JD: Yes, I have certain things of Quintana's. I have, for example, some school uniforms and the pinafore she wore for volunteering at St. John's Hospital in Santa Monica. Now those are things that I feel very warm when I look at. I wouldn't want to live in a house that didn't have room for those. So they'll be around.

TG: You have been immersed in death, so do you think with this book published and your reporting kind of done, you'll emerge more?
JD: Oh, I think so. I'm feeling very strongly the need to do something in another vein. I don't know what that vein will be, but I want to find it.

TG: Are you getting any pleasure in life?
JD: Yes.

TG: Good (*laughter*). What's giving you pleasure?
JD: Quite simple things. For example, yesterday I went to a concert, and the music gave me pleasure.

An Evening with Joan Didion

David L. Ulin / 2011

From ALOUD, presented by the Library Foundation of Los Angeles as part of *Pacific Stan-dard Time: Art in L.A. 1945—1980*, November 16, 2011. © 2011 by David L. Ulin. Reprinted by permission.

I'm sure we all have our favorite Joan Didion book. She speaks so deeply to so many of us. Her voice is really the voice we think of when we think about the sixties, especially in Los Angeles. Somebody had asked me why Joan Didion for Pacific Standard Time. And, well, she never tuned out. She kept her lens, her steady gaze on the American counterculture, on politics, on the Black Panthers, on rock 'n' roll. She told us about ourselves and our culture. She's been called the canary in the American coal mine. She's pre-scient. She's a soothsayer. And we're very very delighted to have her here tonight.

I think this cathedral is exactly the right place to hear Joan Didion because her voice has that clarion quality like a bell in this beautiful cam-panelli up here.

In *Blue Nights*, Joan Didion enumerates memories of her family life here in southern California, in Hollywood, in Brentwood, in Malibu. And she actually laments. She says, "How inadequately I appreciated the moment when it was here." I know we will take away our memories from this won-derful night, but please appreciate this moment. And please welcome Joan Didion and David L. Ulin.

David L. Ulin: It's a privilege to be up here with the writer who has meant everything to me. . . . I wanted to start by asking you about [the opening passage of "The White Album"] because it seems to address a number of issues that come up a lot in your writing, both then and now, this issue of improvisation, this issue of narrative breakdown, or the loss of a defining narrative. This has been a factor, as you say, from the mid-sixties in your work, going back to *Slouching Towards Bethlehem* to "Some Dreamers of the Golden Dream." I wondered if we can talk a little bit about how that sense of broken narrative began to assert itself and how you began to have to think about that as a factor in your writing.

Joan Didion: Well, it began to assert itself during that very period. There was a lot of stuff going on that really did not lend itself, as I said, to any narrative that I knew. So I kept trying to find a new narrative and couldn't. And finally I kind of learned to live without a narrative, which is the coward's way out.

Ulin: Or, I actually think it's the brave person's way in, in some way. Because that notion that you talk about later about narrative being sentimental in some way, something we tend to cling to. We need narrative, but in the end as you say, "We tell ourselves stories in order to live." Or we do for a while. At a certain point those narratives end up deserting us. And I also wanted to start with that because it draws a through line from your earlier work to your new book, *Blue Nights*, which I think is also in some ways a book about when narrative becomes atomized. So I wonder if you can talk a bit about how the new book deals with that question. You say it's a book about your daughter's death, and that's not the narrative we're supposed to hear. The narrative we're supposed to hear is not the one in which the child predeceases the parent. So in terms of approaching that material, I'm curious about your sense of that.

Didion: This was a very difficult book for me to write, actually, because it has no narrative. I didn't find the narrative. I simply decided to go without a narrative, so it was a little tricky for me to write it.

Ulin: Well, it operates as a collection of fragments in some way.
Didion: It's all fragments.

Ulin: You wrote it over a period of six, eight months?
Didion: I wrote it over a period of, I think, six months, yeah.

Ulin: And how did that fragmentary structure evolve? Did you start writing it in fragmentary chunks, or did it at some point become clear to you that was going to be the way through the material?
Didion: I started writing it thinking it was going to be about children in a much more researched way, then it became clear to me gradually that it wasn't about children, it was about my own child. It was about my own

experience. And then I kind of hit a dead spot, where I couldn't see what I was doing, and then the idea of calling it *Blue Nights* occurred to me, and that kind of pushed it through.

Ulin: For those who haven't read it, do you want to explain the blue nights metaphor?

Didion: Blue nights are those nights around the summer solstice when everything turns blue. Well, it doesn't happen in southern California because in southern California the sun just drops. I watched it this afternoon. It just drops into the horizon. But it does happen in New York. It happens dramatically in Europe. But it happens pretty dramatically in New York, too. It's far enough south, or far enough whatever you have to be to get the blue nights. And the blue nights came to represent for me at some point death—the approach of death, the end of the brightness, the coming of the darkness, which of course are ways of thinking about death. So when I realized that I could call it *Blue Nights* I knew it was going to have to do with death, it was going to have to do with getting older. And that was novel to me because nobody had told me I was ever going to get older. So thinking about that kind of kept me going through the period when I was going to abandon the book.

Ulin: You talk in the book both about your own sense of getting older—there's a part where a doctor says to you, "You're not adjusting well to the idea of getting older," and you say, "Adjusting well? I'm not adjusting at all."

Didion: I'm not adjusting, yeah. As somebody always says to me, "It's not for sissies." The idea of getting older was always something that was going to happen to other people, as I saw it.

Ulin: In that sense, I think this is the first book of yours that you really pull out and address the reader directly.

Didion: You have to address the reader directly if you're going to tell the reader your deepest secrets. If I'm going to sit here and tell you how old I am, that's a pretty deep secret, you know. Until I just blew it by writing it down in a book.

Ulin: But you also talk about the difficulty of writing the book. The book in many ways is about both your own process of aging and your process of dealing with Quintana's death.

Didion: It turned out they were the same thing.

Ulin: Can you talk about how they were the same thing, what that means to you?

Didion: They were the same thing because, like aging, Quintana's death wasn't supposed to happen.

Ulin: It's a disruption of the narrative.

Didion: It's a disruption of the narrative.

Ulin: But it's interesting because Quintana is almost a kind of absence at the center of the book. You write a lot about her, but it's really about her absence. And you talk at one point in the book about the difficulty you're having in actually writing about her or addressing her.

Didion: Well, I had difficulty on a couple of levels. When you're writing about a real person you have to work yourself into a feeling that you can, that you have the right to write about that person. And that's a very hard right to justify. And so I had to kind of fight my way past that. I specifically did not talk about Quintana in the last book I wrote, about John's death. I didn't talk about Quintana because it wasn't her book, was my feeling. She could tell her own story. Suddenly it came to then that I did have to tell her story, and I plunged into it.

Ulin: You talked at one point about the question of permission in terms of telling that story.

Didion: Well, there were a lot of aspects of Quintana's life—for example, she was adopted—that got into, "Did I have the right to tell her story from her point of view?" And further, "Did I have the right to tell her story from the point of view of her other parents, who I didn't know and had never met?" That was a quite thorny question that I spent about six months trying to get used to. Finally, like everything else in life, you just plunge ahead and do it willy-nilly.

Ulin: And just see how it works out.

Didion: Just see how it works out.

Ulin: Now, this book and *The Year of Magical Thinking,* and in a lot of ways I think also *Where I Was From,* function as a set. You shift your focus in some way from you looking out and telling other people's stories to you looking inward more and telling your own stories. I'm curious about that shift. When you first started working on *Where I Was From*, how did you make that move from the reporter's position to the memoirist's position?

Didion: That wasn't really a memoir, and I don't think of the two later books as memoir. It says Memoir on the Library of Congress card, I think, but I argued about this with Knopf, actually.

Ulin: What was the substance of that argument?

Didion: I kept saying, "I don't like the word *memoir*. It's soft."

Ulin: Too touchy feely.

Didion: Too touchy feely, yeah.

Ulin: I always found it sort of ridiculous that nonfiction books have to have that signifier at all.

Didion: You can call it nonfiction, which is how I thought of it. What I had wanted to do in *Where I Was From* is I had wanted to write a book about California, but the only way I could come at California was, again, by simply plunging in and telling a lot stories I knew about California. In some cases retelling and trying to find the narrative by trying to find the lies. The untruths. All the untruths I had ever told myself or that anybody had ever told me about California, beginning with my parents and continuing right through the whole package. I think we all, if we grow up in California, get told a lot of untrue things. So I started writing those things down. Then I realized I had told as many untrue things about California as anybody else. So it was a really exciting realization when I realized I could take my first novel and tear it apart, because it was full of lies. The reason I got into that was it was kind of a new way of writing for me, it was not straight looking for the narrative, which I'd always spent my entire adult life doing, it was tearing apart the narrative I had found. It was a different approach.

Ulin: But related in some way, right. Because at the heart of all of it is the sense of breaking apart the false narrative. One of the lines of yours I've used in classes and everywhere is from *Slouching*, that as a writer you're always selling someone out, or that your presence as a reporter in their living room is counter to their best interest. Would you say that your presence in your own living room was counter to your own best interests?

Didion: Sure it is. Where I've pushed myself now is I've torn apart the only narrative I knew. So I'm always having to start with a blank mind. Yes, it is counter to my own best interest.

Ulin: But the writer wins and does it anyway?

Didion: The writer has to win and do it anyway.

Ulin: One of the questions I've been asked about this book when I've talked about it with people is, "Was there ever a moment when you thought about writing a book like this and not sharing it?" You know, writing it for yourself. Is there a sense of being a public writer versus being private writer?

Didion: A lot of people asked me that about *Magical Thinking*. I've never written anything that wasn't for a reader. I cannot imagine writing not for a reader. Some sense of why that might be came through to me when I was watching the rehearsals of *Year of Magical Thinking* when it was made into a play—I say when it was made into a play, *I* made it into a play—there was a point when I was watching the rehearsals for the first time that I realized a play was a collaboration between the audience and the people who were on the stage. And that it came out of a very active collaboration and that it changed every night. That was a kind of fascinating thing which is equally true of writing. Everything you write is a collaboration with the reader.

Ulin: So you don't keep a diary or a journal?

Didion: No, I've never kept a diary.

Ulin: I want to touch a little more on this, then I want to shift into broader questions. I think the first time I read the book, I think I overlooked the aspect of it, or minimized the aspect of it, that is you wrestling with what I think you perceive as your own failings or regrets—maybe *regrets* isn't the right word—about parenting. You have a great line, "I do not know many people who think they have succeeded as parents." This certainly speaks to my sense of my own parenting experience and the experience of most of the people I know who have kids. And the more I think about the book the more that line seems to be important in terms of the story you're trying to tell.

Didion: That was very much the story I was trying to tell when I started the book. But then I realized gradually that wasn't the book I was writing. That wasn't the story I was telling.

Ulin: What was the story you were telling?

Didion: The story I was telling had to do with the blue nights. With death. The approach of some final moment.

Ulin: You talk in the book also about losing your own creative power, or your own literary power, about the idea that your sentences become shorter and more compact. At a certain point there's a line where you say, "I'm telling you this true story to prove that I still can." And I wonder about that to. On reading it, the language seems very focused and forceful. Maybe more stripped down and spare than some of the other books.

Didion: I think it's much more stripped down. I felt it very strongly, that this was a different story. But on the other hand, maybe I've felt it before too. Who knows.

Ulin: You wrote *The Year of Magical Thinking* in, I think, eighty-eight days.

Didion: Yeah, I wrote it in a very short time because I didn't start writing it until—John died on December 30, 2003, and Quintana was already sick but she got sicker during the next four or five months, so obviously I didn't start writing a book at that moment. I didn't start until the fall, and I finished in the fall, so it was a very short time.

Ulin: And in that book I really had the sense reading it that you were writing it as a way of maintaining your sanity.

Didion: I had lost my sanity. I was totally crazy. And I think a lot of people who go through grief experiences are totally crazy, and nobody acknowledges that they're crazy. But they secretly know it.

Ulin: This book, though, obviously, because it was written after the fact, a shorter book over a longer span, for its immediacy it's also got a bit more distance. I'm curious if you can talk a little bit about the distance in that process. Both of them are dealing with tragic circumstances, but one in the white hot center of the moment and one with four, five years of perspective.

Didion: I don't know other than *Magical Thinking* was fast to write not only because I was determined to write it fast because I was determined to finish it within a year of John's death and not much was left of that year, so that was one reason that it was fast. The other reason was because it just seemed to tell itself. This book didn't tell itself. I had to wrestle it out. In retrospect it was kind of exhilarating to keep finding that it was about new things to me. It was a discovery process.

Ulin: You say—and this may tie in with the whole notion of it not being a memoir—you say, "Memories are what you no longer want to remember." The book is a memory book in many ways. It's a litany of memories and you kind of going back over the memories. I wonder if you can talk a little bit about that idea of memories being what you don't want to remember and how that plays into your process through this material.

Didion: Well, memories are what you don't want to remember because they hurt very often. Clearly. Memories are, on the other hand, what you have to remember, also because they hurt. Memories are stunningly tricky that way. Things you think you will never forget you've forgotten before you could say them. It's a kind of scary process, what we remember and what we don't.

Ulin: And how we remember, right, because they're seductive. In some ways it makes me think about what you were just saying about California. Memories can kind of reshape themselves. One of the things that's interesting about this book is watching you try and parse those memories and not allow them to become sentimentalized in a certain way.

Didion: And not without killing them.

Ulin: I want to ask you about this process, both in *Blue Nights* and also in other works. Here [in *Blue Nights*] you're operating both as a kind of observer and the observed, like we were talking about. In works like "Some Dreamers of the Golden Dream" or "Slouching Towards Bethlehem" you were really in the piece as the observer, whether overtly or covertly. You're always allowing us to see both what you're looking at and in some way you as you're looking at it. And I want to ask you about that.

Didion: Yeah, it's kind of important to me, it has been. I thought it was important always for the reader for me to place myself in the piece so that the reader knew where I was, the reader knew who was talking. So I was always putting myself rather more front and center than was approved practice. At the time I started doing these pieces it was not considered a good thing for writers to put themselves front and center, but I had this strong feeling you had to place yourself there and tell the reader who that was at the other end of the voice.

Ulin: How did you develop that idea? There were other writers at the time who were developing sympathetic approaches, you know, the so-called New Journalists. But how did you begin to develop that idea? And how did you sell that in the early days, say, to a magazine like the *Saturday Evening Post*?

Didion: Well, you could sell anything to the *Saturday Evening Post*, frankly. They were going broke. They would try anything.

Ulin: They were a precursor to the print culture today. But as a writer how did you begin to develop that as a strategy?

Didion: It just always seemed essential to me that the reader know where I was. I have no idea how it became so important, but it did.

Ulin: In some of those early pieces that sense of your own perspective became a kind of mechanism by which people either constructed for themselves or thought you were constructing a mythology of California. I think about, say, the opening of "Some Dreamers," where you go through that long riff about "this is the California where . . ." It clearly is coming from your perspective, but it seemed to take on this larger social vision.

Didion: I and the *Saturday Evening Post* almost got sued for that piece. It turned out, when they did the depositions, that all of the stuff the San Bernardino Chamber of Commerce wanted to sue me over came out of Chamber of Commerce literature.

Ulin: But that's an interesting piece because it's ostensibly a magazine piece about a murder trial.

Didion: That's exactly what it is, it's nothing more than a magazine piece about a murder trial, but it was kind of fun to write. I remember John went with me to San Bernadino to check it.

Ulin: To check it in what sense?

Didion: Obviously before it was published I had to check the quotes and the trial. And I had to go over to San Bernadino and spend a day in the lawyer's office, the lawyer who had defended Lucille Miller. But the reason I had to go over to San Bernadino was to check the quotes against his transcript. But anyway, we went over and spent the day in San Bernadino and on the way back stopped at Dodgers Stadium and watched the twilight and it was really fun. And I can't tell you why I brought that up. But as opposed to memories that make you unhappy, it's a nice memory.

Ulin: But it's interesting because it is a magazine piece about a murder trial, but it becomes or seems to want to become something bigger about two Californias. You have the coastal California that everybody thinks of, and you have this more hard-scrabble inland California.

Didion: Right, the California nobody knew.

Ulin: Now obviously you're very identified with kind of a certain vision of California, a certain sense of how postwar California works. I'm curious what your thoughts are on that. I know what my thoughts are. People who've read or written about your work think about it. But in terms of that framing of California, is that something you were ever thinking about consciously, or was that simply where the stories were?

Didion: I was thinking about it consciously. I realized when I was doing *Where I Was From* that I had misunderstood a lot of that stuff.

Ulin: Do you want to talk more specifically about what you had misunderstood?

Didion: I hadn't realized the extent to which the California of my imagination had never really existed.

Ulin: And that's the old—

Didion: That's the old Oregon Trail California that I came from, I thought. Well, I did come from, but it didn't mean what I had thought it meant.

Ulin: What had you thought it meant, and what did you come to think it meant?

Didion: I thought the Oregon Trail California was a better way of life. I thought that it was somehow a nobler way of life. I hadn't realized the extent to which it was permeated with untruths. I didn't realize it really until not long before I did that book about California.

Ulin: So in some ways again it was another collapse of the narrative.

Didion: It was a total collapse of the narrative. Something I wrote about in that book that has stuck in my mind still as a symbol of my misunderstanding of everything: we had a family graveyard outside Sacramento, and I used to go out there and look at the graves, and they were all names familiar to me. Obviously no one I knew, since they were all dead and had been dead since before I was born. But at some point this family graveyard started to be vandalized, and the vandalization got reported in the paper, and a group of neighbors got together and cleaned it up, and my mother reported this to me, and I said, "Didn't somebody in the family do that?" And she said, "No, no. So and so did it." And I said, "I thought he owned it." And she said, "I guess he sold it." It was the selling of what I had preferred to think of as heritage. I saw that it was not too different from the southern Pacific; it was not too different from a lot of California stories.

Ulin: Is that why you called the book *Where I Was From*? The past tense, is that because you're putting away that story?

Didion: Yes.

Ulin: And this is something that I think comes out in the early fiction. In *Run River*, which you take apart in *Where I Was From*, a novel which takes place in Sacramento. And *Play It As It Lays*, which is as much as anything an L.A. novel. I think of Maria driving those freeways as a metaphor for the disconnection of the city. Is there a relationship when you were writing fiction dealing with California and nonfiction dealing with California? Were you doing certain things in one and certain things in the other?

Didion: No, it's the same person. The same person is writing one thing one day and one thing with the other hand. I never could separate stuff.

Ulin: Was it easier to get at certain things in—

Didion: Fiction. It was easier to get at certain things in nonfiction I discovered later.

Ulin: Can you elaborate on that?

Didion: How much easier it is to get at certain things in nonfiction? Well, you can do anything in nonfiction. You can only do one thing in fiction. You can do one thing to different degrees of success. And so when you're writing you just try to make it work better, to make it more successful, but essentially it's always the same thing that you're doing. Nonfiction you can really just, talk about plunging in, you just plunge in and you can go anywhere.

Ulin: You mean, because of the narrative requirements of fiction as opposed to—

Didion: Yeah.

Ulin: Although *Play It As It Lays* is written in a lot of short chapters and has that same kind of jangly, fragmentary energy in a certain sense as some of the essays, but you feel the overriding pull of the story is something you can't get away from in the same way you can in nonfiction?

Didion: I couldn't get away from it in fiction. Even my last novel was what I think of as my Iran-Contra novel. It was a book based on the actual facts of the Iran-Contra case. If it had a single image it was the Hasenfus plane falling out of the sky in Central America—Hasenfus was the pilot—the falling of that plane was what exposed the Iran-Contra finally. Even in that book, which got as close to being nonfiction fiction as you could get, I guess—or as close as I could get—it seemed to me that I would be a lot better off if I could just move it into nonfiction. I'd have more room.

Ulin: That novel came out in 1996. Is that why you haven't written anymore fiction?

Didion: Yeah. I didn't not want to write another novel after that.

Ulin: You talked at one point about taking notes for a novel.

Didion: I still have those notes. They're in a box. I actually am going to look at them as soon as things quiet down after Christmas and see if there's anything in them.

Ulin: The other thing I just want to touch on quickly. For a lot of readers, myself included, one of the things your nonfiction did was to undercut a certain myth of the sixties in California. If you think of a piece like "Slouching Towards Bethlehem," which really is an on-the-ground report from Haight-Ashbury in the Summer of Love, a devastating report, it completely undercuts the flower-child myth that was being sold in the media. I think also in terms of the sort of Edenic qualities of L.A. as the sun and surf capital of the universe in pieces that deal with fire season and fires and floods. In "Los Angeles Notebook" you talk about L.A.'s defining image of itself is of the city on fire. I wanted to ask you about the importance of the sixties or of writing out of the sixties and trying to be a clear-eyed social observer in a time that was so hyped on itself.

Didion: Yeah, you had to keep writing in the sixties because people were telling so many wrong stories you could hardly keep up with them. It was kind of staggering.

Ulin: In some ways we're in a similar moment.

Didion: I think we are in a similar moment. I wonder about a lot of what's going on in public life. I wonder where it's going. And I don't have really hopeful thoughts about it either.

Ulin: No, I don't either. And it's interesting. As I was preparing this interview and reading your work, I came across this line from "On the Morning After the Sixties" from *The White Album*. This was a piece that was published in 1970 originally. And I'm just going to read the last sentence, which is: "If I could believe that going to a barricade would affect man's fate in the slightest I would go to that barricade, and quite often I wish that I could, but it would be less than honest to say that I expect to happen upon such a happy ending." So given what's happened at the barricades in the last twenty-four hours, I think that's—I don't want to say prescient because that struck me three weeks ago when I came across it again—but it does feel like we're in that kind of moment.

Didion: Yeah, and where it will take us is hard to know.

Ulin: And that sense of California as a kind of dangerous landscape. You say in the new book that California is dangerous, not necessarily fatal, but dangerous. And you talk about the notion of when you lived in Malibu the sign was "when the fire comes" not "if the fire comes," that we know these things are coming, that there is something lurking out there no matter how smooth or placid the surface might be that's coming for us at some point.

Didion: Well because I grew up here I was very focused in on the immanence of natural disaster, of fires, of earthquakes, they were always right out there, I could touch them. I don't think you could grow up in California and not have a strong sense that the apocalyptic moment is upon us.

Ulin: I totally agree, as someone who did not grow up in California but moved here. That's not the wrong story, but it does stand in opposition to this other story that we're constantly hearing about California. . . . In some ways it seems to me that a lot of your work is about how do we live in the shadow of that kind of, whether emotional or physical sort of—

Didion: It's the great question of all religions: How do you live with certain annihilation?

Ulin: Yeah, how do you live?

Didion: Yeah. Well, on that note.

Audience member: My question is why you think people have this belief that there is this narrative, why we believe we deserve a narrative. And if there's so much evidence to the contrary that tragedy is going to strike and religions deal with how we're going to move forward, how that relates to our construct of narrative.

Didion: Why we believe we deserve a narrative is another question altogether. The answer to that question is we tell ourselves stories in order to live.

Audience member: You said earlier that you always write for an audience and that hit me because I always feel when I'm reading your stuff that you're writing for me. It feels really personal. And I was just wondering what you imagine when you're writing to your audience? Is it a person?

Didion: It's nobody I visualize. It's a definite person, but I don't visualize that person. It's the reader. The reader is, I can only think, like the audience is to an actor. It's the person you're doing it for.

Ulin: It's the occupying of the public space.
Didion: Yeah.

Audience member: When I was in line outside I was standing with two other writers, and one has been writing for less time than I have and one has been writing for more. The one who's been writing for less said when she writes she feels like a fraud. I asked the one who's been writing for longer, "Did you ever stop feeling like that?" And she said no. Then the person who's been writing for less time asked what it is about Joan Didion's writing, and I said she writes with authority. Where do you get that authority?
Didion: Where do you get the authority? Gradually you get it. You get it from the reader. The reader gives you the authority. It's that feedback. But you don't get it right away. And I always fear that you can lose it unless you're really careful with it.

Ulin: Do you ever feel like a fraud still?
Didion: I don't feel like a fraud, but I feel like someone who hasn't done as much work as she should.

Audience member: I was wondering what the name of your Bouvier des Flandres was?
Didion: He had a fancy name given him by his breeder, but he was called Casey.

Ulin: I have one question that was submitted on Facebook, which is: What is your favorite place in Los Angeles and why?
Didion: Well, I think this [the library] has to be my new favorite place in Los Angeles. There are a lot of places I love in Los Angeles. When I first moved to New York, I came back to Los Angeles for the California primary, and I went to a rally in South Central, and I remember weeping all the way from LAX on my way to this political rally. And I could only think I was weeping because it was so beautiful. But I mean LAX to South Central is not one of the scenic drives of Los Angeles, but it was beautiful that night.

Audience member: One word jumped out when you described the first moment you saw Quintana, "her fierce, dark hair." And that word resonated as I read through the whole book. And listening to you talk tonight I think of all the gifts you've given us over the years and the *fierce* self-reflection is what I'm holding in my heart right now. How did you learn to be so fiercely self-reflective?

Didion: I don't know. I think some people simply criticize themselves more than other people. I had that tendency.

Audience member: On the book cover of *The Year of Magical Thinking* the "John" was in a different color. And on *Blue Nights* it says, "no." What does "no" mean?

Didion: It doesn't mean anything. The same designer did the cover and I don't know what she had in mind, but she didn't tell me. So I can only think it didn't mean anything.

Audience member: I was hoping it meant, No, Quintana didn't die.

Didion: No, it didn't mean that. I wish it did too.

Audience member: I was just wondering what type of advice you have for younger writers just starting out.

Didion: It would take me a week and a half to even begin to answer what I would teach younger writers. You know what I would tell them, I would tell them, "Rewrite. Don't be afraid to rewrite."

Joan Didion

Sheila Heti / 2012

From *The Believer,* online exclusive. © 2012 by Sheila Heti. Reprinted by permission.

"With writing, I don't think it's performing a character, really, if the character you're preforming is yourself. I don't see that as playing a role. It's just appearing in public."

Places to go:
Dark or difficult places
Home
Underwater

One Thursday at noon in December 2011, I spoke to Joan Didion over the phone. She was in a hotel in Washington. The woman at the front desk asked, "Who do you want? Bibion? B as in boy?" I replied, "No, d as in dog," feeling weird and a little hostile. "D as in dog, i, d as in dog, i, o, n." I did not like having to put dog *in Joan Didion's name. And I did not want to speak to Joan Bibion.*

Knopf had given us half an hour to talk. Didion was on book tour for her latest work, the memoir Blue Nights. *She would be appearing at a bookstore later that day.*

I imagined her sitting on the edge of a neatly made bed. I imagined that after we hung up, she would move things about the room, then open the door to another reporter. Or perhaps she would have time to stroll around Washington, take a few hours for herself.

I had been reading only her for the past few weeks: her novels; her essays, collected in We Tell Ourselves Stories in Order to Live; Blue Nights, *written in the wake of her daughter's death from an influenza gone awry, a book about aging and loss and being a mother; and her previous book, the best-selling* The Year of Magical Thinking, *which was about the death of her husband, the writer John Gregory Dunne. That book returned Joan Didion to the center of America's conversation about itself, a place she has spent serious time since the 1960s, when she first began publishing.*

She was born in 1934, and has written like no other about California (where her family lived for generations), and like no other about the profound changes in America in the sixties and seventies, and about political campaigns, and about being a human. In her famous essay "On Self-Respect" she says: "If we do not respect ourselves, we are on the one hand forced to despise those who have so few resources as to consort with us, so little perception as to remain blind to our fatal weaknesses. On the other, we are peculiarly in thrall to everyone we see, curiously determined to live out—since our self-image is untenable—their false notions of us . . . We play roles doomed to failure before they are begun, each defeat generating fresh despair at the urgency of divining and meeting the next demand made upon us."

I quote this only to say that I felt like I was talking to a person not in anyone's thrall, not living out anyone's false notion of her. There was no pose. Her voice was tremendously sensitive—the tiniest inflections seemed to carry a depth of feeling and perception, and a commitment to neither exaggerate nor underplay nor bend the truth to the right or the left; a rigorous person, yet somehow entirely at ease.

I. Performing

THE BELIEVER: I want to start with something you said in the *Paris Review*. When you were a little girl you wanted to be an actress, not a writer?
JOAN DIDION: Right.

BLVR: But you said it's OK, because writing is in some ways a performance. When you're writing, are you performing a character?
JD: You're not even a character. You're doing a performance. Somehow writing has always seemed to me to have an element of performance.

BLVR: What is the nature of that performance? I mean, an actor performs a character—
JD: Sometimes an actor performs a character, but sometimes an actor just performs. With writing, I don't think it's performing a character, really, if the character you're performing is yourself. I don't see that as playing a role. It's just appearing in public.

BLVR: Appearing in public and sort of saying lines—
JD: But not somebody else's lines. Your lines. "Look at me—this is me" is, I think, what you're saying.

BLVR: And do you feel like that "me" is a pretty stable thing, or unstable? Is it consistent through one's life as a writer?
JD: I think it develops into a fairly stable thing over time. I think it's not at all stable at first. But then you kind of grow into the role you have made for yourself.

BLVR: How would you gauge the distance between the role you have made for yourself—
JD:—and the real person?

BLVR: Yeah.
JD: Well, I don't know. The real person becomes the role you have made for yourself.

BLVR: And are you performing for yourself or performing for others?
JD: Performing for yourself. But also, obviously, other people are involved. I mean, the reader is your audience.

BLVR: How much of the work would you say is created in collaboration or in response to an audience?
JD: Oh, I think a lot of it. I did a play based on *The Year of Magical Thinking*, and I was struck by the extent to which the audience became part of the play when it was in performance. The audience was very strongly a part of what went on on the stage. And I think that is also true when you're writing.

BLVR: But in the case of writing, the reader is more your imagination of the reader.
JD: Well, it's not your imagination of the reader—yes, I guess it is your imagination of the reader because the reader isn't physically there the way the audience is in a theater. But it's just as real a collaboration, I think.

BLVR: So what does the reader brings to the collaboration?
JD: Well, the same thing an audience brings to an actor. I can't imagine writing if I didn't have a reader. Any more than an actor can imagine acting without an audience.

BLVR: They're almost born at the same time—writing and the idea of a reader.
JD: Yeah, it simply doesn't exist in a vacuum. If you aren't aware of the reader, you're working in a vacuum.

II. Beginning to Write

BLVR: Do you remember beginning to write?
JD: It was as a child. I was four or five, and my mother gave me a big black tablet, because I kept complaining that I was bored. She said, "Then write something. Then you can read it." In fact, I had just learned to read, so this was a thrilling kind of moment. The idea that I could write something—and then read it!

BLVR: Have you gotten pleasure from reading your own writing?
JD: Over the years, yes. Not always, but sometimes.

BLVR: How would you characterize the kind of pleasure one gets from reading one's own writing when it's good?
JD: Well, it's just a deep pleasure to read something you've written yourself—if and when you like it. Just as it's not a deep pleasure if you don't like it.

BLVR: And do you feel alienated from any particular period of your work?
JD: I never felt close to my first novel, because it simply—I didn't know how to do it, I didn't know how to do what I had in mind. I wanted to mix up the time frame in a way that I was not experienced enough to know how to do, so I eventually did what the editor suggested, and forgot trying to mix up the time frame, and did a very conventional narrative. And that was not a good feeling.

BLVR: The book wasn't close to your vision?
JD: No, it was totally opposite.

III. Getting the Confidence

BLVR: You've said in the past that you don't have a strong sense of reality. You've had a lot of criticism about yourself as a reporter, or have conveyed the feeling that it wasn't naturally what you were. Yet that journalism that you did early in your career, and later in your career, is so strong. When you look back at your essays, do you feel like that is somebody who saw reality, or is it something else?

JD: I think it's somebody who saw reality. But it's also something else. I don't know. This is a touchy—not touchy, but it's a difficult thing to separate those thoughts out.

BLVR: I imagine it would be difficult to write nonfiction, because you have to have such an authority to say, "This is what the world is." How can you really have the authority to say, "I know enough and I've seen enough to be able to conclude things about the world"?

JD: Well, you have to just gain that confidence. Which is part of what you do over the course of your whole career. I mean, you become confident that you have—this sounds ridiculous, but you become confident that you have the answer.

BLVR: Do you remember the point—
JD:—at which you get that confidence?

BLVR: Well, for you.
JD: For me it probably occurred fairly late, when I started getting feedback from the audience. Feedback in terms of a response. Well, it wasn't fairly late. It was fairly early [*laughs*] when I started getting a response from the audience, otherwise I wouldn't have had the nerve to continue.

BLVR: And where would you situate that? Around which book, say?
JD: I would say it happened at *Play It As It Lays*. Which was, when? My third book. And I remember my husband saying, when *Play It As It Lays* was about to come out, "This isn't going to—you're never going to—you're never going to—this book isn't going to make it." And I didn't think it was going to make it, either. And suddenly it did make it, in a minor way. And from that time on I had more confidence.

BLVR: Why did you both feel like it wasn't going to make it?
JD: Because it was my third book and I had not made it until then. And you don't see—I mean, you don't think in terms of suddenly making it. You think you have some stable talent which will show no matter what you're writing, and if it doesn't seem to be getting across to the audience once, you can't imagine that moment when it suddenly will.

BLVR: *Play It As It Lays* was fiction, but that confidence translated into other kinds of writing as well.

JD: Yeah. What happened was I started doing a lot of reporting that gradually came to get noticed, so I was asked to do other things. Gradually, gradually you gain that confidence. Well, you know. You've been through this.

BLVR: Yes, it's gradual. It stuck in my head when your husband said, "It's not going to make it." Did that hurt your feelings to hear that, or was that simply the way—

JD: No, it didn't hurt my feelings. It was, I thought, a realistic assessment. Which I certainly agreed with.

BLVR: What was the first sign that there was going to be a real response?

JD: I don't remember exactly what it was, but suddenly people were talking about this book. Not in a huge way, but in a way that I hadn't experienced before.

BLVR: Did it change your relationship to the book? Did it make you feel more separate from it or anything?

JD: No, it didn't make me feel more separate from it. It made me feel good. It made me feel closer to it. Closer to it. I was so unhappy writing that book because it was just a very hard book for me to write, and I didn't realize until I finished it how depressed it had made me to write it. Then I finished it and suddenly it was like having something lifted from the top of my head, you know? Suddenly I was a happy person.

BLVR: It always happens, for me, that I have a certain attitude toward the world for the time-period I'm writing a book—

JD: Right. You borrow the mood of the book in some way.

BLVR: It's hard to find a book that's safe to write. Because one always goes to dark or difficult places.

JD: Exactly. Sometimes you don't want to go there.

BLVR: But then where can you go? I mean, it's the only place to go, right?

JD: Right.

IV. Woody Allen's "Relationships"

BLVR: In the seventies, you wrote a fascinating article about Woody Allen's movies—including *Annie Hall* and *Manhattan*—which was published in the *New York Review of Books*, where you put "relationships" in quotation marks so much—

JD: I think because he was always talking about *relationships*, quote unquote.

BLVR: But how does it come out of the quotation marks, or how does it get into the quotation marks? Reading the essay, I got the feeling you were saying that the idea of a relationship is something that the culture invented.

JD: It's not something that the culture invented. It was the specific way Woody Allen was using relationships at the time that didn't seem to me to be quite honest.

BLVR: How was it not honest?

JD: I mean, I saw those movies, and people were talking about relationships in them, and that's all that was happening. It just didn't work for me.

BLVR: It was an interesting piece for me to read, because those were the first movies I saw. My father's a huge Woody Allen fan, and to me they seemed like reality, because *Annie Hall* and *Manhattan* were the first times I saw adult life depicted. I must have seen those movies a hundred times in my childhood. So reading your essay was like this light going off, like: Oh, this is just one person's artistic interpretation of life, it's not necessarily—

JD: Not necessarily the whole deal.

BLVR: Yeah, and not documentary. Do you feel like the culture did go in that direction a lot more, where—

JD: Well, it did, after. It became kind of the acceptable way of looking at the world.

BLVR: Something more transient about human relations?

JD: Yeah.

V. Extreme or Doomed Commitments

BLVR: I want to ask you about the idea of the "extreme or doomed commitment." You have a line in *The White Album* where you say, "I came into adult

life equipped with an essentially romantic ethic," believing "that salvation lay in extreme and doomed commitments."
JD: Right.

BLVR: I wonder if you consider marriage or motherhood, or even writing—
JD: I did consider marriage and motherhood extreme and doomed commitments. Not out of any experience of them as such, but it was simply the way I looked at things.

BLVR: And having experienced motherhood and marriage, do you still see them as extreme and doomed commitments?
JD: No, I don't. I mean, not—I don't. I see them as, well, certainly they were for me a kind of salvation.

BLVR: Salvation from what?
JD: From a loneliness, an aloneness.

BLVR: Because the relationship was so intimate, or just the fact of marriage?
JD: Just having another person, answering to another person, was very—it was novel to me, and it turned out to be kind of great.

VI. Finding No Narrative

BLVR: The fragmentation of *Blue Nights* made me think of your essay "Slouching Towards Bethlehem," in which you talk about the reason that these kids are the way they are is because they don't have—
JD: Right.

BLVR:—any aunts and uncles—
JD: Right.

BLVR: And I wonder, as a human and as a writer, if you don't have the same people around you, not just family but also friends, also landmarks in a city that you've lived in for many years—because cities change—does one become more fragmented-feeling, more atomized?
JD: Well, I think you do, and then you have to learn to deal with that. I mean, that was part of what I was doing in this book. This book was quite personal. I don't mean it was personal because I talked about things in my

life that were personal; I mean it was personal in that I was dealing with my own inability to find the narrative.

BLVR: So what does it feel like to come out of a book you've written that doesn't have a narrative?
JD: Well, it's not an encouraging attitude, but at this moment, I wanted to flat-out deal with the fact that I did not have, at the moment, an encouraging attitude. [*Laughs*]

BLVR: Writing something fragmented as opposed to narrative, was it a different kind of thinking?
JD: Absolutely, it was a different kind of thinking. Because what you're normally doing as a writer is trying to find the narrative. And a lot of the pieces I've written over the past ten years or so have had to do with finding the narrative. This was exactly the opposite. This book proceeds from the idea that the narrative isn't there and it's not going to matter.

BLVR: So where is the intensity of the thinking located, then, if not in finding the narrative?
JD: Well, in the idea that narrative doesn't matter, I guess.

BLVR: Does that feel more true to you than being able to find a narrative? Is that a deeper truth?
JD: At the moment it seems so to me, yes. That's kind of what this turned out to be about.

BLVR: Do you feel like if you hadn't written the book, that truth would sort of be hovering, but not fully realized in you?
JD: Yes. Writing is always a way, for me, of coming to some sort of understanding that I can't reach otherwise.

BLVR: How do you think writing works to bring one to an understanding?
JD: You mean how does it bring one to an understanding that one can't reach by some other method?

BLVR: Yeah.
JD: It forces you to think. It forces you to work the thing through. Nothing comes to us out of the blue, very easily, you know. So if you want to

understand what you're thinking, you kind of have to work it through and write it. And the only way to work it through, for me, is to write it.

BLVR: I guess that has probably been true your whole life.
JD: Yeah, it has.

VII. After Christmas

BLVR: In what you're going to write next or what you're writing now, is—
JD: I'm not writing now. I wish I were. I haven't written—I have to do something. I'm going to write a couple of pieces next, but I can't seem to focus in on them. In the spring, I'm going to try to focus in on something.

BLVR: Something assigned to you or something you come up with yourself?
JD: Well, eventually you always have to come up with it yourself. It began with something that was suggested to me by an editor, but part of the process will be trying to translate it into something I came up with myself.

BLVR: Does it feel different to live when you're not working on something?
JD: It feels very different. I don't like it.

BLVR: Does it feel kind of like—for me it feels mushy.
JD: Mushy, loose in the world, yeah. I can hardly wait to get home. I'm going home tomorrow, on a train, and I have to go to California next week, so I'll be gone again. When I think about when my life will be normal again, it's basically after Christmas.

BLVR: So all you're doing is looking forward to After Christmas right now?
JD: I am focusing on After Christmas. That's my narrative. [*Laughs*]

BLVR: And that's when things will settle down, you'll be able to sit at a desk and so on.
JD: Sit at a desk, and in the same place every day, yes.

BLVR: And that's more vividly living?
JD: Yeah.

VIII. Finding the Rhythm

BLVR: When do you feel like you're most writing?
JD: When I'm finding the rhythm.

BLVR: Are there times when you're writing when you feel like you're evading writing?
JD: Of course there are times. There must be times when everybody writes when they feel they're evading writing.

BLVR: And what is the nature of the evasion? Not thinking?
JD: Not thinking, yeah. Not thinking.

IX. A Lifetime of Magical Thinking

BLVR: You called your previous book *The Year of Magical Thinking*, and in your essay "Sentimental Journeys" you said that New Yorkers, in trying to recover from a highly publicized rape, relied on certain "magical gestures," thinking it could affect their fate. I wonder if you have some sense of what makes us so superstitious? Is it about hope or a lack of control, or why we are such deeply superstitious creatures? We can't even get away from it.
JD: No, we can't. Well, I think it's just part of the way we are programmed.

BLVR: What does it ultimately give us, do you think?
JD: Well, ultimately it gives us a narrative, I guess. There seems to be no way around it. We need one. And it's a sad moment when you can't find one.

BLVR: When you look back on your life, is its narrative the narrative you literally wrote yourself?
JD: Yes, I would say it was.

X. The Bottom of the Sea

BLVR: Do you think if you hadn't written, hadn't been a writer, could there have been some completely other—

JD: Oh, I wonder. I wanted to be an oceanographer, actually. And when I was out of school and living in New York and working for a magazine, I actually went out to the Scripps Institute, which is now UC San Diego, but then it was just the Scripps Institution of Oceanography, run by the University of California, and I asked them what I would have to do to become an ocean-ographer. And basically they said I would have to go back to high school, you know. I hadn't taken any of the science courses that would enable me to take the science courses that I would need to take in order to go to . . . any place. So I abandoned the idea of being an oceanographer, but I can see myself still as an oceanographer, if I could get to that point.

BLVR: Does it seem like a happier life?
JD: A happier life? I don't know. I've liked being a writer.

BLVR: It's a different way of going underwater.
JD: It's a way of going underwater, yes. Well, I've always been interested in how deep it was, you know.

Index

Printed in Great Britain
by Amazon

67479199R00111